CONTENTS

DEDICATION

❧

This book of *"Food, Fun & Laughter"*
is dedicated to everyone who enjoys entertaining
friends and family in homes
filled with love, laughter and home cooking.

❧

Expression of Appreciation

❧

My sincere appreciation
to everyone who contributed in any way
to help make this book possible.
My warm-hearted thank you to all of you.

INTRODUCTION

Dear Friends,

What a joy it has been to put together this book of easy recipes, thoughts for the day, and humor that I call, *"Food, Fun & Laughter"*. What pleasant memories I have of sitting down with family and friends to delicious home cooked meals... talking and laughing together... After all, humor is healthy! It is important for our physical, emotional and Spiritual health. My desire for this book is that you will enjoy the select delicious, easy to prepare recipes and that it will bring laughter to your family and friends... Remember, what the heart gives away is never gone, but is kept in the hearts of others.

With the numerous letters and compliments I have received on my first cookbook, you have inspired me with this book, *so:*

*I'd like to introduce you
to this little book.
I hope you will like it
for the time it took.*

*The way to a man's heart
is through the stomach they say.
So let's get busy
without delay.*

*There's sweets and meats,
there's all kinds of treats.
There's something for a party,
or for the family that eats hardy.*

*There's breads and rolls
and cookies too.
So let's begin to plan
without much ado.*

*There's salads and dressings,
soup and main dishes you see.
You can plan a meal
for the fam a le.*

*There's frosting, cookies
and all kinds of cakes,
just about anything
you'd want to make.*

*So take these recipes
we've gotten together,
And cook with pride
in fair or foul weather.*

*And don't forget
laughter has been added,
For that seems to be what
the World needs and is after.*

MEMORIES

of Happy Times
are Treasured Souvenirs...

Bill, Greg, Brad, Jim, Tim and Doug

Beverages
Appetizers
&
Dips

FROM MY HEART

From my heart, I do wish this book
to be the answer for you when you feel lonely
and need a lift, on one of those ordinary days in your life,
for it was through prayer and inspiration
that this book has been possible.
It is my desire that this book will not only reveal
my love to share excellent recipes and humor
for your enjoyment and pleasure,
but also my love for Jesus Christ.
Knowing him as my personal Savior
has brought me much joy and satisfaction.
I have met so many wonderful people
through my cookbooks and consider that
such a great blessing...

A FRIEND IS A GIFT

LAMENTATIONS 3:23
Gods promises are new every morning.
Great is his faithfulness.

These recipes are Delicious, Easy and Quick,
and will meet the need for any occasion. *Enjoy!*

CELEBRATION PUNCH

1 large can apricot juice   2 cups water
1 large can pineapple   ½ cup orange juice
  juice   ⅓ cup lemon juice
1 bottle cranberry juice   1½ cups sugar

Mix all ingredients, then add large bottle of 7 Up before serving. ½ gallon sherbet of your choice can be added. Serves 60 people.

CREAMY PUNCH

2 packages orange   1 large bottle 7 Up
  Kool-Aid, mix well   1 quart pineapple
  with sugar   sherbet
1 46 ounce can
  pineapple juice

Mix ingredients together. Change color of Kool-Aid for different color punch. (Lime, cherry, etc.)

The seeds planted today
will be the flowers of tomorrow.

A MIRACLE OF FRIENDSHIP
There's a miracle called Friendship
that dwells within the heart
and you don't know how it happens
or when it gets a start
but the happiness it brings you
always gives a special lift
and you realize that friendship
is one of God's precious gifts.

FRIENDSHIP TEA

An appreciated gift for any occasion.

1 18 ounce jar orange
   flavored instant
   breakfast drink
1 cup sugar
¼ cup presweetened
   lemonade mix

¼ cup instant tea
1 3 ounce package
   apricot gelatin
3 teaspoons cinnamon

Combine all ingredients in a large bowl, mixing well. Store in airtight containers. To serve, place 1½ tablespoons mix in a cup. Add 1 cup boiling water and stir well. Yield: About 50 cups.

PEACH MILK SHAKES

Delicious!

1 cup fresh peaches,
   peeled and diced
½ cups honey

1½ cup milk
1 pint ice cream *or*
   yogurt

Celebrate each day!

FLING IT OUT—
When a bit of kindness hits ye,
After passing of a cloud,
When a bit of laughter gits ye,
An 'yer spine is feeling proud,
Don't forget to up and fling it
At a soul that's feeling blue,
For the moment that you sling it,
It's a boomerang to you.

CRANBERRY PUNCH

A great punch. Add orange slices before serving.

1 12 ounce can frozen
   orange juice
3 cups pineapple juice
1½ quarts water

1 6 ounce can
   frozen lemonade
6 pints cranberry
   juice cocktail

Mix all ingredients. Serves 50 people.

For a refreshing drink, mix a half glass cranberry juice and a half glass of 7 Up.

ICED TEA

1 family size tea bag *or*
   4 regular

¾ cup sugar
1½ quarts water

Bring 1½ cups water to a boil. Remove from stove and add tea bag. Cover with lid and let steep for 4 minutes. Then add to the remaining water and sugar that has been mixed in pitcher. Pour over ice in tall glasses. May garnish with lemon wedges. (For stronger tea, use less water.)

The way I see it, if you want the rainbow,
you gotta put up with the rain.

MOM'S COUNTRY LEMONADE

This is lemonade at it's best, the old fashioned way!

1 cup freshly squeezed lemon juice	**ice cubes**
¾ cup sugar	**4 cups cold water**
	1 lemon, thinly sliced

Combine lemon juice and sugar in large pitcher. Stir to dissolve sugar. Add water, lemon slices and ice cubes. Blend well. Makes 6 servings. Wonderful, beats any mix too!

FRUIT PUNCH

1 12 ounce can frozen orange juice	**2 quarts 7 Up**
1 46 ounce can pineapple juice	**1 6 ounce can frozen lemonade**

Combine all ingredients. Chill well.

*Friendship is precious
and adds sunshine to life.*

HOT CIDER PUNCH

½ **gallon apple cider** *or*   ⅓ **cup brown sugar**
   apple juice   2 **teaspoons Allspice**
4 **cinnamon sticks**

Mix together well. Keep hot in crock pot.

WASSAIL

½ **gallon apple juice**   2 **teaspoons Allspice**
1 **quart cranberry juice** ¼ **cup lemon juice**
1 **cup orange juice**   ⅓ **cup sugar**
5 **cinnamon sticks**

Combine juice and sugar in percolator. Put spices in the coffee grounds container and allow to go through perk cycle. A crock pot can be used. Serve hot. ENJOY!

EGGNOG

2 eggs
1 small package vanilla
   instant pudding

1 teaspoon vanilla
6 cups milk
⅓ cup sugar

Beat all together, except milk. Add milk. Refrigerate. Sprinkle with nutmeg or cinnamon to taste when serving.

CONCENTRATE ON JOY
*Lord, help me
to concentrate on joy.
Let me think positive every day...
and not worry
or hold onto old resentments.
Increase my faith,
let me conquer fear.
Thy will be done.
I am sure with Your help,
my joyful heart
will be at peace.*

*JOY IS...BIBLICAL
JOY IS...A CHOICE
JOY IS...HAPPINESS
JOY IS...FREE BUT NOT CHEAP
JOY IS...THE BEST OPTION
JOY IS...BASED ON WHO YOU ARE,
   NOT ON WHAT YOU HAVE*

Just when you thought you were winning the rat race,
along come faster rats.

DILLED WEED DIP

1 cup mayonnaise	1 tablespoon
1 cup sour cream	grated onion
1 teaspoon parsley	1 teaspoon dill weed
flakes	

Mix ingredients and refrigerate overnight. Serve with raw vegetables. Yield: 1¼ cups.

MEXICAN BEAN DIP

Quick, easy and yummy!

2 16 ounce cans	1 package taco
refried beans	seasoning
1 16 ounce container	1 large bag
sour cream	plain Tostitos
1½ cups grated	
cheddar cheese	

In bowl, mix refried beans and taco seasoning. Spread in a 9" x 13" pan. Spread sour cream on top of beans, then sprinkle cheese on top of sour cream. Bake at 350° for 30 minutes. Dip Tostitos in dip.

TASTY 2 INGREDIENT DIP

1 can chili con-carni   **Small box**
                             Velveeta cheese

Heat together in a miniature crock pot and enjoy with chips.

PSALM 55:22
Cast thy burden up on the Lord
and he shall sustain thee;
he shall never suffer the righteous to be moved.

BAKED VIDALIA ONION DIP

Simply delicious!

2 cups vidalia onions,   **2 cups mozzarella**
chopped   **cheese, shredded**
                              1¾ cups mayonnaise

Stir all together. Place in flat baking dish. Bake for 30 minutes in a 350° oven. Serve with favorite chips.

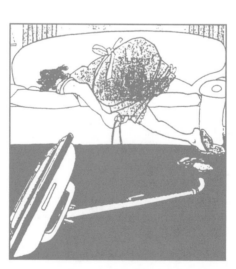

Every once in while the handles of responsibility
get the best of Gertie!

DELICIOUS CHEESE BALL

2   8 ounce cream cheese
1   8 ounce can crushed
      pineapple, drained
1   tablespoon season
      all salt, *or* McCormick
      Salad Supreme

⅓ cup chopped pecans
¼ cup chopped
      green pepper

Let cream cheese stand at room temperature to soften. Cream the cheese slowly. Add rest of ingredients and form into a ball. Roll in ½ cup pecans and refrigerate.

SPINACH DIP

1   package frozen
      spinach, drained well
1   medium onion
1   cup mayonnaise

1   package Knorr's
      vegetable soup mix
1   can water chestnuts,
      drained and chopped

Mix all ingredients and chill for several hours or overnight. Serve with favorite crackers. Can be used for tea sandwiches. Will keep in refrigerator for 2 weeks.

Hint: Use imitation sour cream and Weight Watchers mayonnaise to cut those calories. Very tasty!

RECIPE FOR LIFE AND HAPPINESS
Good Thoughts
Consideration for Others
Generosity
Kind Deeds
Forgiveness
Laughter

Mix well daily. Add Faith and Hope.
Serve generously to everyone you meet.

Cheerfulness is a sign of a Happy Heart!

DELICIOUS DIP

1 15 ounce jar
    pimento cheese
	1 tablespoon
	    chopped parsley

1 2 ounce can
    deviled ham
	1 teaspoon
	    minced onion

½ cup mayonnaise	4 drops Tabasco sauce

Use either fresh or dried parsley flakes. Beat all ingredients with mixer to blend. Chill.

SALMON DIP

2 cans canned salmon	½ cup chili sauce
1 pint sour cream	1 envelope Lipton Onion Soup mix
2 tablespoons prepared mustard	

Drain salmon well. Remove skin and bones. Mix all ingredients together. Chill overnight. Serve with chips or crackers. It is super with large corn chips!

When you can't say a word, you can pray.

SHRIMP DIP

1 6½ ounce can deveined
  shrimp, drained
1 8 ounce package
  cream cheese, softened
1 cup salad dressing

1 teaspoon grated onion
½ teaspoon lemon juice
  dash of Tabasco sauce
  enough chili sauce
  to make mixture pink

Mash up shrimp in a medium bowl. Add all remaining ingredients. Chill thoroughly. If too firm, add a bit of salad dressing to soften. Serve with chips, crackers or fresh vegetable sticks.

MAKE A JOYFUL NOISE!

BEEF DIP

1 8 ounce package
  cream cheese, softened
1 3 ounce package
  corned beef
2 teaspoons minced
  onion

2 tablespoons
  mayonnaise
¼ cup jar filled
  pimento *or*
  green olives *or*
¼ cup green pepper

Blend all ingredients well and refrigerate overnight to allow flavors to blend. Serve with sesame crackers or another favorite.

God Bless You!

TACO CHIP DIP

½ pound ground chuck, browned
1 16 ounce sour cream
1 package taco seasoning
1 large can refried beans

lettuce
tomato
olives
shredded cheddar cheese

First layer: Refried beans.
Second layer: Mix sour cream and taco seasoning together and spread on refried beans. Top with chopped lettuce, tomato and cheese. Optional: Black olives, etc.

CLAM DIP

1 8 ounce package cream cheese
3 tablespoons clam juice
1 can drained clams, after reserving juice

1 teaspoon lemon juice
2 teaspoons Worcestershire sauce
dash pepper *and* garlic salt

Combine all ingredients with fork, then mix with electric mixer. Serve with Fritos or carrots, celery, etc.

You can smile when you can't say a word...

QUICK FRUIT DIP

**1 8 ounce package
strawberry flavored
cream cheese**

**1 large marshmallow
topping**

Blend softened cream cheese with marshmallow topping.
Serve with fresh fruit such as sliced apples, oranges, strawberries, grapes, etc.

*Every day holds a possibility
of a miracle.*

PICKLED BEETS

Easy and adds much to a table and one's meal!

½ **cup vinegar**
¼ **cup water**
⅓ **cup sugar**

½ **teaspoon salt**
2 **cups cooked,
sliced beets**

Heat vinegar and water to boiling. Add sugar and salt. Blend
until mixed and let mixture boil again. Pour mixture over
sliced beets; let stand overnight. Chill before serving.

LAYERED MEXICAN DIP

Easy to put together and delicious!

1st layer:
  1 can refried beans
2nd layer:
  1 cup sour cream
  1 cup mayonnaise
  1 package taco seasoning,
    mixed together
3rd layer:
  1 ripe avocado, mashed
4th layer:
  1 can picante sauce

5th layer:
  grated cheddar *or*
  mozzarella cheese
6th layer:
  chopped green onions
7th layer:
  chopped tomatoes
8th layer:
  sliced black olives

Refrigerate...serve with Mexican chips.

MATT. 11:28-30

Come unto me, all ye that labor and are heavy laden
and I will give you rest. Take my yoke upon you,
and learn of me; for I am meek and lowly in heart;
and you shall find rest unto your souls.

Brighten the corner where you are!

MARSHMALLOW FRUIT DIP

8 ounces cream cheese ¼ cup orange juice
1 small jar
marshmallow cream

Mix softened cream cheese, marshmallow cream and orange juice well. Serve with fresh fruit.

BEST DEVILED EGGS

Great for an appetizer
or served with a regular meal.

6 hard cooked eggs 1 teaspoon vinegar
¼ cup salad dressing 1 teaspoon prepared
2 tablespoons   mustard
  chopped onion ⅛ teaspoon salt
2 tablespoons   dash of pepper
  pickle relish   paprika

Slice eggs in half lengthwise, carefully remove yolks. Mash yolks with salad dressing. Add remaining ingredients, except paprika; stir well. Stuff eggs whites with yolk mixture. Garnish with paprika.

CRISPY CHICKEN STICKS

Great for an appetizer or prepare more for a meal.

2 skinless, boneless
  medium chicken
  breasts
1 tablespoon grated
  parmesan cheese

⅓ cup cornflake crumbs
¼ cup yellow cornmeal
⅓ cup flour
  nonstick spray coating

Rinse chicken, pat dry with paper towels. Cut chicken into pieces about 1"x 3½". In a shallow bowl combine cornflake crumbs, corn meal and parmesan cheese. Dip each chicken piece in flour, then in a little water. Roll in cornmeal mixture to coat. Spray a baking sheet with nonstick coating. Place chicken on the baking sheet. Bake in a 350° oven for 20–25 minutes or until tender and no longer pink...ENJOY!

Your Joy is Contagious!

DILLED CRACKERS

A great snacking cracker!

1 box oyster crackers
1 package Hidden Valley
  Ranch dressing mix
½ teaspoon dillweed

½ teaspoon lemon
  pepper
⅓ cup salad oil

Warm oil, then mix in oyster crackers until coated with oil. Mix dressing mix, dillweed and lemon pepper. Add to crackers, a little at a time. Mix thoroughly to coat. Sore in covered container.

BAR-B-Q MEATBALLS

Great for an appetizer.
Make miniature ones, serving with toothpicks.

Meatballs:
1½ pounds ground chuck
¾ cup oatmeal *or*
  bread crumbs
6 tablespoons
  chopped onion
1 tablespoon
  worcestershire sauce
  salt *and* pepper

Sauce:
4 tablespoons
  brown sugar
1 cup catsup
1 cup milk
½ cup water
1 tablespoon
  worcestershire sauce

Meatballs:
Mix the above into meatballs and roll in flour. Brown in frying pan and drain. Put in baking dish.

Sauce:
Mix sauce ingredients and heat. Pour sauce over meatballs in baking dish. Bake in 350° oven for 20–25 minutes. Miniature meatballs may take slightly less time.

POTATO SKIN CRISPS

2 baking potatoes

8 tablespoons
  parmesan cheese

Bake potatoes for 1 hour in a preheated 400° oven. Let cool, then cut into quarters. Scoop out the potato and use in another dish. Sprinkle the inside of each shell with parmesan cheese. Place potatoes on a cookie sheet and brown under the broiler for 3–5 minutes. Top with any desired topping. Good with melted cheddar cheese and bacon.

BROCCOLI CHEESE BREAD

store brand frozen   1 cup shredded
bread dough   cheddar cheese
1½ cups broccoli, cooked   1 egg white
and cut into pieces

Thaw bread according to package instructions. Flour coun-
tertop and roll out bread dough. Spread broccoli and cheese
down center of rolled-out dough. Smear egg white around
edges of bread dough. Fold bread dough over broccoli and
cheese, pinch edges closed and fold ends closed. Put bread
into greased (may use vegetable spray) glass pan seam side
down, cover with plastic wrap and microwave 15 seconds at
a time until bread has risen to about twice it's original size.
Preheat oven to 350°. Brush egg white on top of bread and
bake bread for 15–20 minutes or until golden.

*Roses have thorns
and thorns have roses...*

EASY FRENCH ONION SOUP

1 package Lipton's   1½ tablespoons
Onion Soup   cornstarch
1 egg yolk   mozzarella cheese,
3 tablespoons water   shredded
french bread

Prepare onion soup as directed. While hot, pour into individual dishes. Mix egg yolk with water and 1½ tablespoons cornstarch. Divide this equally into the four dishes. Stir. Top with
a thick slice of french bread and lots of mozzarella cheese.
Put in oven until cheese is mostly melted. Sprinkle with
parmesan cheese if desired.

HEARTY POTATO SOUP

6 cups potatoes,
  peeled and cubed
¼ cup chopped celery
½ cup chopped onion
½ cup diced carrots
1 tablespoon butter
2 teaspoons
  parsley flakes

3 cups milk, divided
1 teaspoon salt
¼ teaspoon pepper
2 chicken
  bouillon cubes
2 cups hot water
¼ cup flour

Combine first eight ingredients in dutch oven. Dissolve bouillon cubes in hot water, add to potato mixture. Bring to a boil over medium heat. Cover and simmer 8 minutes, or until vegetables are tender. Dissolve flour in ¼ cup of the milk, stir into soup. Add remaining milk. Cook on medium heat until thickened, about 20 minutes. Makes 10 servings.

Do you ever feel like just running away FOREVER?

Usually the thought of actually running is enough to change my mind.

JUST FOR FUN

Laughing is the Best Medicine!

A man was asked how he got the bump on his head. He replied,"Well, there was this sign over the entrance to a building and since I'm nearsighted, I stepped closer to read it, and it read, "Caution, door swings out."

There was a person that was so insecure that when the football players were in a huddle, he thought they were talking about him.

When someone asked me my favorite color, I said plaid.

It takes some people 90 minutes to watch 60 minutes.

When the doctor asked me if I had trouble make decisions, I told him,"Well, yes and no."

I was put in the hospital when I was struck by a thought.

A sign in a store read — "Shoplifters will be cheerfully beaten to a pulp, regardless of race, color, creed or national origin...HAVE A NICE DAY!"

Did you see the bumper sticker that read,"Don't tell me what kind of a day to have."

Why did the fellow jump up and down before taking his medicine?
Because the label said, "Shake well before using".

Why did the fellow stand on his head in the kitchen? Because he was making an upside down cake.

Did you see the bumper sticker that said,"I may rise, but I refuse to shine."

Did you hear about the couple who married for better or for worse? He couldn't do any better and she couldn't do any worse.

Salads

METRIC

System & Conversions

SYSTEM
Weight
1 kilogram=1000 grams
1 hectogram=100 grams
1 dekagram=10 grams
1 gram=1 gram
1 decigram=.1 gram
1 centigram-=.01 gram
1 milligram=.001 gram

Volume
1 hectolitre=100 litres
1 dekalitre=10 litres
1 litre=1 litre
1 decilitre=.1 litre
1 centilitre=.01 litre
1 millilitre=.001 litre

CONVERSION
Volume
1 fluid oz.=29.5 millilitres
1 quart=approx. 1 litre
1 T.=scant 15 millilitres
1 t.=5 millilitres
1 c.=250 millilitres

Weight
1 oz.=approx. 29 grams
1 lb.=approx. 454 grams
1 cup=213 grams margarine (or liquid solids)
1 cup=149 grams flour (or fine powders)
1 cup=202 grams sugar (or granular foods)
1 cup= 106 grams rice (or grains)

·THINGS TO DO TODAY·

1. find the list

FRESH LETTUCE & SPINACH SALAD

A wonderful salad to prepare ahead of time.

1 head of lettuce, broken in small pieces	2 bunches green onions
¾ pound spinach, broken in small pieces	6 hard boiled eggs, diced
2 tomatoes, diced	1 pound fried bacon, crumbled *or* bacon bits
1¼ cups grated cheese	
1 box frozen peas	

Layer salad as given in a 9"x 13" dish. Mix 2 cups mayonnaise, 1 cup sour cream, 1 package Hidden Valley ranch dressing. Spread over salad, sealing edges wells.

OLD FASHIONED LETTUCE AND ONIONS

This recipe is sometimes called "Wilted Lettuce." When preparing this, don't forget the cornbread!

Chop up fresh green onions and lettuce of any variety. Sprinkle with salt. Heat bacon grease in frying pan. Have it real hot. Pour over lettuce and onions and mix well. ENJOY!

In my heart there rings a melody!

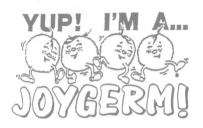

Yup! I really am a "JoyGerm",
And invite you to be one too,
So we can show the love of God,
In all we say and do.
Let's share His love with everyone,
In every place and every way,
Then everyone can be a "JoyGerm"
Living for Him each day!

LEMON TUTTI-FRUTTI

Serve in parfait glasses
with a dollop of whipped topping.

1 large can pineapple chunks	2 bananas, thickly sliced into chunks
1 small can mandarin oranges	½ cup coconut
1 large can fruit cocktail	1 small box instant lemon pudding mix
2 tablespoons lemon juice	

Do not drain fruit. Sprinkle undrained fruit with pudding mix. Stir and chill.

ORANGE-CARROT SALAD

1 small box orange
  gelatin
1 cup boiling water
½ cup water

1 small can crushed
  pineapple, undrained
1 large carrot grated

Dissolve gelatin in boiling water well and then add ½ cup cold water. Chill until partially set. Fold carrots and crushed pineapple into thickened gelatin. Pour into bowl and refrigerate until firm.

FRIENDS ARE COMFY
Friends are the greatest...
especially ones that sparkle inside and out...
like you!

ORANGE—RAISIN SALAD (IN SYRUP)

Another wonderful salad.

6 sweet seedless oranges, peeled and sliced
1 tablespoon lemon juice
walnut pieces

5 tablespoons water
⅓ cup honey
½ cup raisins

Arrange sliced oranges in pretty serving bowl. In a saucepan, combine honey and water. Stir over low heat until honey dissolves. Boil 2 minutes. Add lemon juice and raisins. Boil 5 minutes. Place oil in medium bowl. Pour mixture over oranges, let stand until cool. Cover and refrigerate.

"Last summer we had a family reunion picnic."
"That sounds nice. Who showed up?"
"Five cousins, four grandparents, six uncles,
and about two thousand ants."

"We don't have to be happy to laugh.
Indeed, we become happy because we laugh..."

ORANGE—WALNUT SALAD

A wonderful salad.

Salad:
medium bunch bibb *or*
red leaf lettuce
¼ cup chopped walnuts
sweet & sour dressing

1 orange, sectioned
and cut up in small
pieces, *or*
mandarin oranges
crumbled bleu cheese,
optional

Wash and tear lettuce into bite size pieces. Add nuts and cut up orange sections. Toss with salad dressing. Can divide into salad bowls and sprinkle bleu cheese on top.

Salad dressing:
Mix,
2 to 3 tablespoons sugar
3 tablespoons vinegar

2 tablespoons salad oil
1 teaspoon salt

Stir until sugar dissolves.

Count your blessings
...name them
one by one...

BROCCOLI SALAD

Delicious...

1 bunch fresh broccoli,
chopped in small pieces
10 pieces crispy fried
bacon, crumbled *or*
broken

1 small onion, red *or*
purple, chopped
½ cup sunflower seeds,
kernels
¾ cup raisins, golden

Sauce:
1 cup mayonnaise
¼ cup sugar

2 tablespoons red
wine vinegar

Combine first 4 ingredients, add raisins and sauce. Marinate overnight.

HEBREWS 6:16
*Let us therefore come boldly
unto the throne of grace, that we may obtain mercy
and find grace
to help in time of need.*

WALDORF SALAD

Delicious!

2 cups diced apples
1 cup celery, chopped
½ cup raisins
½ cup walnuts, chopped

¼ cup salad dressing
1 tablespoon sugar
½ teaspoon lemon juice
dash salt

Combine apple, celery, nuts and raisins. Blend in salad dressing, sugar, lemon juice and salt. Fold into apple mixture and chill. Serves 6.

Note: Grapes, bananas or pineapple tidbits and marshmallows are optional.

APPLE SALAD

Salad:
- 6 apples, not peeled, cubed
- 2 stalks celery, chopped
- ½ cup nuts
- 1 cup mini marshmallows
- 2 cups grapes, cut in halves
- 2 bananas, sliced
- raisins, optional

Dressing:
- 4 ounces cream cheese
- ¼ cup sugar
- 1½ cups Cool Whip
- ¼ cup milk
- 1 tablespoon lemon juice
- 1 teaspoon vanilla

Mix all dressing ingredients except Cool Whip. Beat well. Fold in Cool Whip. This may be made early in the day. Mix apples, celery, etc. Just before serving toss with dressing. Like the others, this salad is delicious.

"Where are your 'I told you so' cards?"

> *You can say that again!*
> *"The only medicine that needs no prescription,*
> *has no unpleasant side effects*
> *and cost no money is laughter!"*
>

CRANBERRY SALAD

A great salad to prepare all year long.

1 3 ounce package raspberry Jello	1 8 ounce can crushed pineapple, in syrup
1 can whole cranberry sauce	½ cup chopped pecans 1 apple, peeled and grated

Dissolve Jello in 1 cup boiling water. Stir in cranberry sauce, mixing well. Stir in crushed pineapple, juice and all. Stir in nuts and grated apple. Chill until firm. Save time and prepare the day before.

CHERRY SALAD

An attractive salad,
why not serve in a crystal dish...Yummy!

Salad:

2 3 ounce packages cherry Jello	2 cups boiling water
1 can cherry pie filling	1 small can crushed pineapple

Dissolve Jello in water and add ingredients. Put in a square pyrex dish and congeal. When congealed add topping.

Topping:

1 6 ounce Philadelphia cream cheese	½ cup sour cream
	½ cup sugar

Mix well together. Sprinkle with chopped nuts. Can be made 2 days ahead.

FRUIT SALAD

1 can apricot pie filling
1 cup pineapple tidbits, drained
1 cup sliced strawberries
1 banana, optional, stir in just before serving

1 cup diced red apple
1 cup miniature marshmallows
1 cup fresh diced orange *or* mandarin

Stir well and chill before serving. Easy to prepare and delicious.

FROZEN FRUIT SALAD

Having company? This is the perfect salad to prepare days ahead. Easy to prepare and delicious!

1 can whole cranberry sauce
1 20 ounce can crushed pineapple, drained

¼ cup sugar
4 bananas, chopped

Mix the above in a large bowl. Refrigerate for 45 minutes.

Add:
½ cup chopped nuts   1 18 ounce Cool Whip

Stir well. Put in paper cups in muffin tins; freeze. Take out a few minutes before serving.

Note: Part of this can be frozen in flat glass 8" x 8" dish. You'll love it!

Eat a live toad first thing in the morning and nothing worse can happen to you the rest of the day!

POTATO SALAD

Homemade potato salad is very tasty. Serve often!

3 large potatoes	½ cup mayonnaise
½ cup chopped celery	½ cup sour cream
½ cup chopped onion	1 tablespoon sugar
2 hard boiled eggs, chopped	1 tablespoon mustard
1⅓ cups chopped green pepper	¼ cup relish

Boil potatoes in lightly salted water until tender; let cool. Dice potatoes and eggs, combine with remaining ingredients. Chill.

Housework done properly can kill you—

Have A HAPPY DAY

ARTICHOKE—RICE SALAD

1 package Chicken Rice-A-Roni	½ chopped green pepper
2 jars marinated artichoke hearts	¼ teaspoon curry powder
8 pimento olives, sliced oil from 1 jar artichokes	2 chopped green onions
	½ cup mayonnaise

Cook the Rice-A-Roni as directed and cool. Cut up the artichoke hearts. Mix all ingredients together and add salt and pepper to taste. For something different, try it, you might like it!!!

BLACK–EYED–PEA SALAD

2 15.8 ounce cans
black eyed peas
1 cup green pepper
½ cup onions
1 small jar sliced
mushrooms, drained
¾ cup mayonnaise

2 teaspoons vinegar
2 teaspoons sugar
1 cup chopped celery
3 hard boiled eggs,
chopped
1 small jar diced
pimiento, drained

Combine ingredients in a large bowl, tossing gently. Cover and chill well.

FRUIT SALAD SAUCE

Truly delicious...

1 cup sugar
juice of 1 orange *and*
½ teaspoon grated peel
juice of 1 lemon *and*
½ teaspoon grated peel
dash salt

2 beaten eggs
5 teaspoons cornstarch
1 cup pineapple juice
1 8 ounce cream cheese

Combine all ingredients, except cream cheese. Cook until thick, stirring with wooden spoon. Chill until cool. Whip the cream cheese and fold the other mixture into it. Serve over fresh fruit.

1 PETER 5:7
*Cast all your anxiety on him
because he cares for you.*

CELERY SEED DRESSING

1 teaspoon grated onion
½ teaspoon dry mustard
2 tablespoons
  cider vinegar
2 more tablespoons
  vinegar

½ cup sugar
1 teaspoon salt
1 cup salad oil
1 teaspoon celery seed

Mix first 5 ingredients with electric mixer. Slowly pour in salad oil, beating constantly. Add 2 more tablespoons vinegar and celery seed and blend well. Store in refrigerator.

PRETZEL SALAD

2 cups crushed pretzels
3 tablespoons plus
¾ cup sugar
1 stick margarine

1 large strawberry Jello
2 small packages
  frozen strawberries
1 8 ounce Cool Whip

Cream margarine and 3 tablespoons sugar. Add 1¾ cups pretzels. Put in 9" x 13" pan. Cool 350° until lightly browned. Mix cream cheese, Cool Whip and ¾ cup sugar. Spread over pretzels. Dissolve Jello with 2 cups boiling water. Add ½ cup cold water. Add strawberries and juice. Set aside and gel. Spread over cream cheese mixture. Sprinkle with pretzels.

Stress?
No Problem!
"When I take good care of body, mind, and spirit —
and nurture my sense of humor —
I'm in control of myself, whatever may happen.
Then, when stress comes, I simply say, Hello stress.
Thanks for the challenge!"

ANNETTA'S FROZEN SURPRISE

This is a delicious recipe.
You can use fruit cocktail in place of fruit
if you do not have all fruits available.

2 peaches
3 large bananas
1 large can pineapple
   tidbits, drained
2 tablespoons sugar
1 cup grapes

1 can cherry pie filling
1 cup mini
   marshmallows
1 large carton
   Cool Whip

Mix together the first two ingredients, then add fruit. Stir in
Cool Whip. Pour into large flat dish, or two 9" glass dishes.
Freeze. As you desire, take out of freezer and cut in slices,
dipping out with spatula.

When we start to count flowers,
We cease to count weeds.
When we start to count blessings,
We cease to count needs.
When we start to count laughter,
We cease to count tears.
When we count happy memories,
We cease to count years.

COLESLAW

After trying this recipe, you will agree,
homemade is best!

3 pounds head cabbage,
   shredded
2 carrots, grated
2 green peppers, diced

2 tablespoons vinegar
⅓ cup sugar
1⅔ cups salad dressing

Combine cabbage, carrots and green peppers together in
large bowl. Mix vinegar, sugar and salad dressing together in
small bowl and mix well. Add to vegetables and mix together
well. Chill. Mix again before serving.

APPLE FRUIT SALAD

A delicious salad to take to a pot luck!

Fruit:
- 3 apples, cored and chopped
- 2 large bananas
- 1 small bunch grapes
- 1 cup miniature marshmallows
- 1 cup nuts
- 1 cup crushed pineapple, drained

Dressing:
- 1 cup pineapple juice
- 1 egg, beaten
- 2 tablespoons flour
- ¾ cup sugar

Drain pineapple juice and put into a measuring cup. Add water to juice to equal 1 cup liquid. Add other 3 ingredients for dressing into small saucepan. Bring to a boil and stir until thick. Cool. You can refrigerate while preparing the fruit. Put all remaining ingredients into large mixing bowl. Pour dressing over fruit and mix well. Chill at least 1 hour before serving.

COTTAGE CHEESE SALAD

This is a surprisingly great salad.

- 1 pound cottage cheese
- ¼ teaspoon salt
- pepper to taste

- 1 each: tomato, onion *and* green pepper
- scant ½ cup Miracle Whip *mixed with*
- 2 tablespoons sugar

Mix all ingredients. Let chill well or set overnight.

PINEAPPLE PISTACHIO SALAD

A salad you can put together in minutes.

1 3½ ounce package instant pistachio pudding
1 cup miniature marshmallows
1 small can mandarin oranges
½ cup maraschino cherries
1 small carton small curd cottage cheese
1 small can crushed pineapple
1 13½ ounce frozen whipped topping

Mix all ingredients together. Chill well before serving.

*Serving salads in a clear bowl
makes a very pretty dish!*

FIVE CUP SALAD

1 cup sour cream
1 cup coconut
1 cup mandarin oranges
1 cup miniature marshmallows
1 cup crushed pineapple, drained

Place all ingredients in a bowl and mix well. Chill.

1 TIMOTHY 6:8
And having food and raiment let us be content.

THREE BEAN SALAD

Will keep when refrigerated for several days.

1 pound can green
beans, drained
1 pound can yellow
wax beans, drained
1 pound can light red
kidney beans, drained
½ cup chopped green
pepper
½ cup finely chopped
onion

Marinade:
¼ cup sugar
⅔ cup vinegar
⅓ cup vegetable oil
1½ teaspoons salt
½ teaspoon pepper

In a large bowl combine the beans, pepper and onion. In a
quart jar, combine the marinade ingredients. Cover and shake
thoroughly. Pour over bean mixture. Mix together gently.
Chill overnight. Serves 12.

CURE FOR THE BLUES
A laugh a day is healthy,
Get your humor off the shelf.
And as you go about today,
Try laughing at yourself.
With laughing each day,
Your gloom is sure to go away!

*So live that your memories
will be part of your happiness!*

CARROT—RAISIN SALAD

¾ cup carrots, scraped
   and grated
½ cup raisins
¼ cup chopped nuts,
   optional

½ cup mayonnaise
1 teaspoon vinegar
1 tablespoon sugar
⅛ teaspoon lemon juice

Combine carrots, raisins and chopped walnuts in a bowl.
Combine remaining ingredients, stirring well. Add to carrot
mixture. Toss gently. Serves 4.

Grandson Scott, a runner at Texas A&M

CELEBRATE EACH DAY—
Its riches
Its glory
Its pain
Its failures
Its success
Its disappointments
Its excitement
Its sameness

SALMON MACARONI SALAD

1 large can salmon,
  drained and flaked
½ cup green pepper,
  chopped
2 tablespoons onion,
  chopped
4 tablespoons salad
  dressing

2 teaspoons
  worcestershire sauce
1 teaspoon seasoned
  pepper
1 tablespoon
  lemon juice
1 8 ounce package
  elbow macaroni

Combine salmon, green pepper, onion, salad dressing, worcestershire sauce, seasoned pepper and lemon juice in a large bowl. Toss gently to mix. Add hot cooked macaroni, toss gently again to coat ingredients with dressing. Salad can be served at once or refrigerated.

TUNA—MACARONI SALAD

2 cups cooked elbow *or*
  shell macaroni
1 7 ounce can tuna,
  drained and flaked
1 hard cooked egg,
  chopped
½ cup cubed cheddar
  cheese

¾ cup frozen peas
½ cup salad dressing
4 tablespoons pickle
  relish
2 tablespoons
  minced onion

Combine all ingredients. Mix well. Chill. Serve on lettuce leaves.

A smile is a frown turned upside down.

CHICKEN FRUIT SALAD

Can be used as luncheon entree.

2 cups cooked
  chunked chicken
2 cups cooked macaroni
¾ cup pineapple tidbits
1 cup chunked
  cantaloupe *— leave out — Too watery*

1 cup seedless grapes
¼ cup slivered almonds
¼ cup raisins
¼ cup celery

Dressing:
Mix together...
  ½ cup mayonnaise

  1 tablespoon honey *or*
    sugar

Add dressing to all ingredients and mix well. Serve on a bed of lettuce and garnish with strawberries.

GALATIANS 5:22–23
The Fruit of the Spirit is love, joy, peace, long-suffering, gentleness, goodness, faith, meekness, temperance.

HEBREWS 3:13
Encourage one another daily, while it is called today.

ORANGE TAPIOCA SALAD

Children and men like this salad very much.
Good served with any meat.

1 package orange	2 cans pineapple tidbits
tapioca pudding	2 cans mandarin
2 cups pineapple juice	oranges
1 package orange Jello	2 bananas
1¼ cups boiling water	

Cook pudding with 2 cups pineapple juice. Cool. Mix Jello
with 1¼ cups boiling water. Cool. Combine first two mixtures
with pineapple chunks and mandarin oranges. Just before
serving stir in bananas.

CHRISTMAS SALAD

Actually, a good salad to serve anytime!

1 package lime Jello	1 cup nuts
1 cup boiling water	½ cup celery, chopped
1 8 ounce package	1 cup mini
cream cheese	marshmallows
1 small can crushed	1 pint whipping cream
pineapple	

Prepare Jello with water. Set until ready to gel. Add cream
cheese, pineapple, nuts, celery and marshmallows. Mix well.
Chill until almost set, then fold in whipped cream. Cool
Whip can be used in place of whipping cream.

TACO SALAD

How about taking this on a picnic?

Salad:
- 1 head lettuce, chopped
- 1 pound ground chuck
- 1 8 ounce grated cheddar cheese
- 1 small can kidney beans
- 1 large onion, chopped
- 4 tomatoes, chopped
- 1 package taco seasoning

Dressing:
- 1 8 ounce Thousand Island dressing
- ⅓ cup sugar
- 1 tablespoon taco seasoning

Brown ground chuck. Add taco seasoning, reserving 1 table-spoon for dressing. Use a large salad bowl, allowing enough room to toss salad at serving time. Layer salad ingredients in salad bowl, starting with lettuce and ending with cheese. Cover and refrigerate. At serving time, toss salad with dressing and taco chips.

HUG ME QUICK
A hug a day increases the heart rate and circulation and aids in an all-around feeling of being "OK". It is a long established tradition that we need four hugs a day for survival, eight hugs for maintenance, and twelve hugs for growth!

SPAGHETTI SALAD

1 pound cooked
   spaghetti, drained
   and rinsed
1 onion, chopped
1 bottle Italian
   dressing to taste

1 green pepper,
   chopped
1 tomato, chopped
3 tablespoons
   McCormick Salad
   Supreme

Break up spaghetti into small pieces and cook. Combine all ingredients together. Allow to chill several hours overnight.

I Think I'm Having STRESS!

HOT CHICKEN SALAD

Great for a pot luck dinner.

2 cups chicken, cooked	2 teaspoons grated
2 cups diced celery	onion
½ cup slivered almonds	1 cup mayonnaise
½ teaspoon salt	1 tablespoons
½ teaspoon Accent	lemon juice

Mix ingredients. Over top, put 1 cup broken potato chips. Put ½ cup grated cheese on top. Bake in 8" x 8" pan at 375° for 15 minutes if at room temperature...20 minutes if refrigerated. Sometimes you might need to double the recipe.

ORANGE SALAD

A very good salad and will keep well in the refrigerator for several days.

1 small crushed pineapple, strained	1 small orange Jello
	1 cup nuts, optional
1 small Cool Whip	1 small cottage cheese

Mix all and refrigerate until firm. Scoop out and serve.

PHILLIPIANS 4:13
I can do all things through Christ which strengthens me.

JUST FOR FUN

Laughing is the Best Medicine!

A lady walked into a beauty shop, sat down in the chair and asked, "Do you know of anything that would cure a severe case of hiccups?" The beautician walked over to the sink and quietly wrung out a hand towel, came back and smacked the lady over the face with it. The lady said, "What did you do that for?" The beautician replied, "Well, do you still have the hiccups?" The lady answered, "I didn't have the hiccups when I came in here." I came in to use the restroom, but there is someone in the car with a severe case of hiccups, maybe you can go out and try it on her..."

There were three women in the kitchen visiting. One lady went to the door and said, "It sure is windy out there." One of the other ladies spoke up and said, "It isn't Wednesday, its Thursday." The third lady spoke up and said, "Well, I'm thirsty too, I'm going to get up and get us all a drink."

There were three sisters living together. One sister went upstairs and when she reached the top of the stairs said, "What did I come up her for?" The sister sitting at the table said, "Knock on wood, I sure hope I don't get like that." The second sister started up the stairs and couldn't remember if she was getting in or out of the bath tub. The sister sitting at the table started knocking on wood said again, "Hope I don't get like her.......wonder who's at the door?"

A fellow told his doctor that his memory was very bad, that he couldn't remember anything. The doctor said, "When did you first notice it?" The fellow answered, "Notice what?"

Breads
&
Muffins

SIMPLIFIED

Measures

dash — less that ⅛ teaspoon
3 teaspoons — 1 tablespoon
16 tablespoons — 1 cup
1 cup — ½ pint
2 cups — 1 pint

2 pints (4 cups) — 1 quart
4 quarts (liquid) — 1 gallon
8 quarts (solid) — 1 peck
4 pecks — 1 bushel
16 ounces — 1 pound

If you want to measure part-cups by the tablespoon,
remember:

4 tablespoons — ¼ cup
5⅓ tablespoons — ⅓ cup
8 tablespoons — ½ cup
10⅔ tablespoons — ⅔ cup
12 tablespoons — ¾ cup
14 tablespoons — ⅞ cup

A lady was on her way to work and when passing by the bakery window saw a large cinnamon roll in the window. She prayed that if she was supposed to have that cinnamon roll that there would be a place to park in front of the bakery...the 15th time around there was...

NEVER FAIL ROLLS

You'll be happy you tried these.

2 cakes *or* packages yeast	4½ to 5 cups flour
2 cups lukewarm water	½ cup sugar
1 teaspoon sugar	3 eggs
2 teaspoons salt	½ cup melted shortening

Soften yeast in water with 1 teaspoon sugar. Beat with mixer until light and smooth. Add sugar and eggs and beat again until smooth. Beat in another cup of flour, then stir in remaining flour, or enough to make an easily handled dough. Knead well and place in a greased bowl. Cover and set in a warm place to rise until doubled in bulk, about 2 hours or longer. Shape into rolls, and place in well greased pans. Cover and let rise until light, about 20 or 30 minutes. Bake for 20–25 minutes in preheated 375° oven. Can be used for cinnamon rolls. *Note: Use more flour if needed.*

This house is clean enough to be healthy and dirty enough to be happy.

If you want breakfast in bed...
sleep in the kitchen.

OVERNIGHT
FRENCH TOAST CASSEROLE

This makes a lot — real good!

**10 to 16 ounces
cubed French *or*
Italian Bread
(with crust) *or***

**1 to 1 1/2 loaves
Holsum brand
French Toast Bread
(cubed)**

After cubing bread, place into a large or extra large bowl so that it will accommodate the following:

(Use electric hand mixer to blend)
8 to 10 large eggs   **3 teaspoons sugar**
2½ to 3 cups milk   **1 tablespoon vanilla**
1 teaspoon salt

Mix well and pour over cubed bread. Be sure you cover all the bread. If too much liquid, add more bread. Should mixture be too dry, add more milk in small amounts. Let mixture refrigerate for 8–36 hours, stirring every four hours to recoat. Place in a well buttered, greased casserole dish, dot with small pieces of butter. Bake at 350° for 1 hour or until fluffy and golden brown. Dust lightly with powdered sugar and serve with warm syrup.

All of the really valuable things you own
are things you cannot photograph!

BUTTERMILK BISCUITS

When in the mood to go Homemade!

2 **cups all purpose flour**	2 **teaspoons baking**
½ **teaspoon soda**	**powder**
¾ **teaspoon salt**	½ **cup shortening**
	1½ **cups buttermilk**

Preheat oven to 450°. Mix flour, soda, salt and baking powder. Cut in shortening with a pronged fork. Add buttermilk
and mix quickly until dough forms a ball. Turn out on a
floured surface and knead a few times. Pat or roll out to a
½" thickness; then cut with a floured biscuit cutter. Bake
approximately 12 minutes on an ungreased baking sheet.

PROVERBS 11:25
He who refreshes others
will himself be refreshed.

Advertisement in the newspaper:

IRISH SODA BREAD

A delicious hearty bread.

1 cup all-purpose white flour
½ cup whole-wheat flour
2 tablespoons granulated sugar
1 teaspoon baking soda
½ teaspoon vanilla
½ teaspoon salt

½ cup currants
2 teaspoons caraway seeds
¾ cup buttermilk, plus additional for brushing

Preheat oven to 400°. Lightly oil a pie pan or coat it with non-stick cooking spray; set aside. In a large bowl, whisk together flours, sugar, baking soda and salt. Stir in currants and caraway seeds. Make a well in the center of the dry ingredients. Gradually pour in the buttermilk, stirring with a fork just until combined (do not overmix). Turn the dough out onto a lightly floured surface and knead several times. Form into a ball, flatten slightly and place in the prepared pie pan. Brush the top with buttermilk and dust with flour. With a sharp knife, cut a ½" deep X into the top of the loaf. Bake until the loaf is brown on top and sounds hollow when tapped on the bottom, about 30–40 minutes. Let cool slightly before serving.

WHOLE WHEAT BREAD

Fun to make. Share with a shut in.

2 packages dry yeast
½ cup warm water
4 eggs
2 teaspoons salt
¼ cup sugar
¼ cup molasses
½ cup dry milk

⅔ cup vegetable oil
1 cup hot water
2 cups whole
    wheat flour
4 cups white flour
1 teaspoon vanilla

Soak yeast in ½ cup warm water. Beat eggs and add salt, sugar, vanilla, molasses, dry milk, oil and hot water. Add yeast. Stir in flour until it clears the bowl. (Flour is variable so exact amounts may differ.) Turn on to board and knead until smooth ball is formed. Cover with towel and let rise until double in bulk and imprint of 3 fingers stays in. Knead a few minutes. Make into loaves. Let rise nearly to top of pan. Bake at 350° for about 30 minutes. Makes 4 loaves.

❦MOTHER'S RECIPES❦
Most women have a pantry filled
With spices, herbs and stuff,
Salt and sugar, yeast and flour
But that's not quite enough.
My mom's the finest cook on earth
And she told me long ago
That bread's no good unless you add
Some loving to the dough;
"And when you're baking pies," she says
"A pinch of faith and trust.
If added to the shortening makes
A tender, flaky crust;
And compassion by the spoonful
In the batter of a cake,
Makes it come out light and fluffy,
Just the finest you can make."
Now these things can't be purchased
in the store across the way:
But mother keeps them in her heart
And uses them each day.
—Reginald Holmes

I have discovered the secret of happiness —
it is work, either with the hands or the head.
The moment I have something to do, the draughts are
open and my chimney draws, and I am happy.

ZUCCHINI BREAD

One of the best!

3 eggs
¾ cup cooking oil
1½ cups sugar
2 cups chopped
　zucchini
2 teaspoons vanilla
3 cups flour
1 teaspoon salt

1 teaspoon baking soda
½ teaspoon baking
　powder
2 teaspoons cinnamon
¾ cup chopped nuts
¾ cup raisins *or*
　cut up dates

Mix eggs, oil, sugar, zucchini, and vanilla. Sift together dry
ingredients and add to egg mixture. Stir in nuts and/or raisins
or dates if desired. Turn into two greased 8" x 4" loaf pans
and bake at 350° for 50–60 minutes. Makes two medium
loaves.

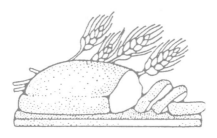

Happiness is like jam...
it's hard to spread even a little
without getting some on yourself!

MONKEY BREAD

5 packages buttermilk
biscuits
1 cup sugar

2 tablespoons cinnamon
¾ to 2 sticks butter

Combine sugar and cinnamon in bowl. Cut biscuits in quarters and roll them in sugar and cinnamon mixture. Put in bundt pan a layer at a time. Occasionally sprinkle sugar and cinnamon mixture between layers until it is all gone. Melt butter and pour over biscuits. Bake at 325° for 30 minutes.

ACTS 16:31
Believe in the Lord Jesus Christ
and you will be saved and thy house.

AMISH FRIENDSHIP
STARTER FOR BREAD I

Fun — Share With Friends!

2 cups flour   1 package dry yeast
2 cups warm water

Use non-metallic bowls and utensils; wooden, plastic, glass.

Day 1: Mix ingredients. Leave out at room temperature, uncovered, or cover with plastic wrap or cheesecloth.

Days 2, 3 & 4: Stir well with wooden spoon.

Day 5: Stir and add 1 cup each of milk, flour and sugar.

Days 6, 7 & 8: Stir well.

Day 9: Same as 5.

Days 10 & 11: Stir well.

Day 12: Ladle 1 cup of starter into each of 4 containers and refrigerate. Use 1 cup to make bread recipe; keep one for later. Give two to friends. If you don't bake that day, add 1 teaspoon sugar; stir and refrigerate. Date the jar and every 10 days, remove the starter; transfer it to a bowl. Add 1 cup each milk, flour and sugar. Leave it on counter for two days; then either bake it or divide it among friends.

FRIENDSHIP BREAD II

1 cup starter
1 cup oil
1 cup sugar
½ cup milk
3 eggs
1 teaspoon vanilla
½ teaspoon
  baking powder

1 teaspoon cinnamon
½ teaspoon baking soda
½ teaspoon salt
1 6 ounce box instant
  vanilla pudding
1 cup chopped nuts,
  optional

Mix first five ingredients; add dry ingredients and mix well.
Put into two well-greased loaf pans. Bake at 350° for 40–50
minutes.

Grandsons Brent and Ryan

MOTHER'S YEAST DONUTS

Precious memories!

1 cake yeast	½ cup sugar
1½ cups milk, scalded	3 tablespoons butter
1 tablespoon sugar	1 teaspoon vanilla
4½ cups sifted flour	1 beaten egg
¼ teaspoon salt	

Dissolve yeast and 1 tablespoon sugar in lukewarm milk. Add 1½ cups of flour and beat well. Cover and set aside to raise 1 hour. Add sugar and butter, which have been creamed. Add well-beaten egg and remainder of flour, vanilla and salt to make moderately stiff dough. Knead lightly and let raise 1½ hours. When light, turn out on floured board, roll to ⅓" thick. Cut with donut cutter, let raise 1 hour. Fry in hot grease with the top side down up in grease...dip in moderately thin powdered sugar glaze, consisting of powdered sugar, milk, a little melted butter and a teaspoon of vanilla.

PHILLIPIANS 4:19
My God shall supply all your needs according to his riches in Glory.

REFRIGERATOR ROLLS

Bake as you desire.

2 packages yeast	2 eggs
2½ cups warm water	2 teaspoons salt
¾ cup soft margarine	8 to 8½ cups flour
¾ cup sugar	1 teaspoon vanilla

Preheat oven to 400°. Dissolve yeast in warm water and add margarine, sugar, beaten eggs, salt, and 4 cups flour and beat well. Add rest of flour and knead for ten minutes. Put in greased bowl, cover tightly, and store in refrigerator. When you want rolls, shape into rolls, let rise, and bake until golden brown or about 15-20 minutes.

When you get wrinkled with care and worry,
it is time to get your faith lifted.

BANANA BREAD

Excellent!

½ cup butter
3 bananas,
  beat into a liquid
2 eggs

2 cups flour
scant cup sugar
1 level teaspoon soda
½ cup chopped nuts

Cream butter and sugar, add eggs and mashed bananas. Sift soda into flour. Mix together and bake at 350° for 45 minutes to 1 hour.

CORNBREAD

Delicious!

1½ cups self-rising
  corn meal
1 cup (8 ounces)
  cream corn,
2 eggs

1 cup sour cream
½ cup oil
hot peppers,
optional

Mix and bake at 425° for approximately 25–30 minutes.

THiNGS
To DO
TODAY:
1. Pick Yourself
   up.
2. DUST Yourself
   off.
3. Start all
   over again.

DILL SEED BREAD

Delicious with cold meats
for open-faced sandwiches.

1 package yeast	2 teaspoons dill seed
¼ cup warm water	1 teaspoon salt
1 cup cottage cheese	¼ teaspoon
2 tablespoons sugar	baking soda
1 tablespoon minced	1 egg
onion *or* onion salt	2¼ to 2½ cups flour
½ teaspoon vanilla	
1 tablespoon melted butter	

Dissolve yeast in warm water. Combine cottage cheese,
sugar, onion, butter, dill seed, salt, soda, egg, vanilla, and yeast.
Add flour, forming stiff dough; beating well after each addition. Cover and let rise until double in size. Knead a little.
Place in well-greased pan and let rise again. Bake at 350° for
40–50 minutes. Brush with butter and sprinkle with salt.

I JOHN 1:9

*If we confess our sins, he is faithful and just
to forgive our sins and to cleanse us
from all unrighteousness.*

PUMPKIN BREAD

Makes a nice gift!

3⅓ cups all-purpose flour
1 teaspoon ground
  cinnamon
½ teaspoon salt
3 cups sugar
1½ cups solid-pack
  pumpkin
⅔ cup chopped nuts

2 teaspoons
  baking soda
1 teaspoon ground
  nutmeg
1 cup vegetable oil
4 eggs
⅔ cup water
⅔ cup raisins

In a large mixing bowl, combine flour, baking soda, cinnamon, nutmeg and salt; set aside. In another bowl, place oil, sugar, eggs, pumpkin and water. Stir into flour mixture. Add nuts and raisins; mix together only until dry ingredients are moistened. Divide batter between two greased 9" x 5" x 3" loaf pans. Bake at 350° for 50–60 minutes or until breads test done. Cool for 10 minutes on wire rack before removing from pans. Makes 2 loaves.

JELLY ROLL

Fun to make, easy! Try it, you'll like it!

4 eggs
¾ cup sugar
¾ teaspoon baking soda

1 teaspoon vanilla
¾ cup flour
¼ teaspoon salt

Beat eggs until light. Gradually add sugar. Beat until creamy, then add vanilla. Sift baking powder with flour and gradually add to egg mixture. Add salt and beat batter until smooth. Line a jelly roll pan or cookie sheet pan with wax paper. Grease it well. Spread the batter in it. Bake in preheated 375° oven for about 13 minutes. While hot, invert on piece of wax paper sprinkled with confectioner's sugar. Spread with jelly. Roll up. Wrap in waxed paper. When cool, cut in slices to serve.

Much happiness is overlooked
because it didn't cost anything...

SOUTHERN
SWEET POTATO PECAN BREAD

1½ cups sifted all-purpose flour	2 teaspoons baking powder
¼ teaspoon salt	1 teaspoon nutmeg
½ teaspoon cinnamon	1 cup sugar
2 eggs, lightly beaten	½ cup vegetable oil
2 tablespoons milk	1 cup mashed, cooked sweet potatoes
1 cup chopped pecans	
½ cup raisins	

Preheat oven to 325°. Grease bottom only of an 8½" x 4½" x 2½" loaf pan. Stir together flour, baking powder, salt and spices in mixing bowl. With a spoon, stir in sugar, eggs, oil and milk; stir to blend. Stir in sweet potatoes, pecans, and raisins. Pour batter into pan. Bake for 1 hour and 10 minutes. Cool for 15 minutes.

REFRIGERATOR MUFFINS

Easy...Delicious...Bake as desired.

5 cups flour	1 cup vegetable oil
4 cups sugar	4 eggs, beaten
4 teaspoons baking soda	2½ cups Grape Nut cereal
2 teaspoons salt	2 teaspoons cinnamon
1 quart buttermilk	

Mix all ingredients together. Fill cup cake holders ¾ full. Bake in preheated 350° oven for 15-20 minutes. Makes 5 dozen.

A husband came home and the house was a mess. The wife said, "What's the matter?" The husband asked what she had been doing all day. She answered, "Well, do you remember this morning, you asked me what I did all day? Well, today I didn't do it!"

BANANA-NUT MUFFINS

Use ripe bananas and you'll be pleasantly surprised with extra-sweet, moist muffins.

½ cup (1 stick) butter *or* margarine, softened
1 cup granulated sugar
2 large eggs
2 large ripe bananas, mashed
2 cups all-purpose flour
1 teaspoon salt
1 teaspoon baking powder
½ teaspoon baking soda
1 cup buttermilk
½ cup chopped pecans
1 teaspoon vanilla extract
2 teaspoons cinnamon

Preheat oven to 400°. Grease 12 standard size muffin pan cups or use paper liners. Beat together butter and sugar at medium speed until light and fluffy. Add eggs, 1 at a time, beating well after each addition. Beat in bananas until smooth. Mix together flour, salt, baking powder, baking soda and cinnamon. Alternately stir flour mixture and buttermilk into egg mixture until dry ingredients are just moistened. Stir in nuts and vanilla. Do not overmix batter; it should not be completely smooth. Spoon batter into prepared pan, filling two-thirds full. Bake until lightly golden 15–18 minutes. Transfer muffin pan cups to a wire rack to cool.

A Kitchen Prayer

God bless this kitchen — its cozy space
Holds both a hearth and gathering place.
May every meal that I prepare
Be seasoned with God's loving care.

APPLE COFFEE CAKE

Make this for coffee hour.
Be sure cake is cold before turning out.
If turned out hot it will break up.

5 tablespoons sugar	2½ teaspoons vanilla
2 teaspoons cinnamon	3 teaspoons
3 cups flour	baking powder
1 cup sugar	1 teaspoon salt
1 cup cooking oil	5 apples, peeled,
4 eggs	cored and sliced thin
¼ cup orange juice	

Combine sugar and cinnamon and set aside. In a large bowl put flour, sugar, oil, eggs, orange juice, vanilla, baking powder and salt. Beat well. Grease 10" tube pan. Pour in one-third of the batter, half the apples, and one-third of the cinnamon and sugar alternately until all ingredients are used. Bake at 350° for 1 hour and 10 minutes.

Smile, God loves you.

HEALTHY APPLE—WALNUT MUFFINS

No added fat or sugar. These tasty muffins
use fruit and buttermilk to keep them moist!

2 cups all-purpose flour
1 teaspoon baking soda
¼ teaspoon ground cinnamon
¼ teaspoon ground ginger
¼ teaspoon ground allspice
¼ rounded teaspoon salt

2 large eggs
1 cup plus 2 tablespoons apple juice
1 teaspoon vanilla
⅔ cup buttermilk
2 tablespoons oat bran
2 tart apples, peeled, cored and chopped
⅓ cup chopped walnuts

Garnish:
1 small tart apple, peeled, cored and cut into 12
thin slices.

Preheat oven to 375°. Grease 12 standard size muffin pan
cups or line with paper liners. Mix together flour, baking
soda, cinnamon, ginger, allspice, nutmeg and salt. Mix together eggs, apple juice and buttermilk. Stir flour mixture and oat
bran into egg mixture until dry ingredients are just moistened. Do not overmix. Gently stir in chopped apples and
nuts. Spoon batter into prepared pan, filling cups two-thirds
full. Garnish each muffin with an apple slice. Bake muffins
until lightly golden and tops spring back when pressed,
about 25 minutes. Transfer pan to wire rack to cool slightly.
Turn muffins out onto rack to cool completely.

GREAT BANANA MUFFINS

Makes 4 dozen muffins.

3 cups all-purpose flour
2 cups granulated sugar
½ teaspoon salt
½ teaspoon baking soda
2 teaspoons ground cinnamon
4 eggs, beaten
1½ cups vegetable oil

1½ teaspoons vanilla extract
1 8 ounce can crushed pineapple, undrained
1 cup chopped walnuts
2 cups very ripe mashed bananas

Preheat oven to 350°. In a large bowl, combine the flour, sugar, salt, soda and cinnamon. Add the eggs and oil and stir until moist. Stir in vanilla, pineapple, nuts and bananas. Spoon into regular muffin cups and bake 20 minutes. Sprinkle with powdered sugar or cool and frost with cream cheese frosting.

*I'm lost.
I've gone to look for
myself. If I should
return before I get back,
please ask me to wait.*

APPLE & OAT BRAN MUFFINS

1¼ cup whole wheat flour
⅓ cup packed
   brown sugar
¼ teaspoon baking
   soda
¼ teaspoon
   ground nutmeg
1 cup buttermilk
2 tablespoons
   cooking oil

1 teaspoon vanilla
1 cup oat bran
2½ teaspoons
   baking powder
¼ teaspoon salt
¼ teaspoon
   ground cinnamon
2 egg whites
¾ cup shredded,
   peeled apple

In a medium bowl, stir together flour, oat bran, brown sugar, baking powder, baking soda, salt, nutmeg and cinnamon; set aside. In a small bowl, combine buttermilk, egg whites and oil. Add to dry ingredients; stir just until moistened. Stir in shredded apples. Store batter tightly covered, in the refrigerator for up to 5 days. To bake, spray muffin cups with nonstick spray coating. Spoon about ¼ cup batter into each muffin cup. Bake in a 375° oven for 18–20 minutes or until a toothpick inserted near center comes out clean. Makes 12 muffins.

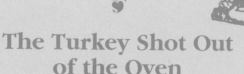

The Turkey Shot Out
of the Oven
Jack Prelutsky

The turkey shot out of the oven
and rocketed into the air;
It knocked every plate off the table
and partly demolished a chair.

It ricocheted into a corner
and burst with a deafening boom;
Then splattered all over the kitchen,
completely obscuring the room.

It stuck to the walls and the windows,
it totally coated the floor;
There was turkey attached to the ceiling
where there'd never been turkey before.

It blanketed every appliance,
it smeared every saucer and bowl;
There wasn't a way I could stop it —
that turkey was out of control!

I scraped and I scrubbed with displeasure,
and thought with chagrin as I mopped
That I'd never again stuff a turkey
with popcorn that hadn't been popped.

gobble!
gobble!

Vegetables
Casseroles
&
Meats

ROASTING

Guide

MEAT	Set Temp.	Time in Minutes per Pound		Time In Minutes per Pound Started Cooking from Frozen State
BEEF				
Standing Rib 6-8 pounds	300°	Rare	18-20	43
		Medium	22-25	47
		Well Done	27-30	55
Less than 6 pounds	300°	Rare	33	55
		Medium	45	60
		Well Done	50	65
Rolled Ribs	300°	Rare	32	53
		Medium	38	57
		Well Done	48	65
Rump (High Quality)				
Standing	300°		25-30	50
Rolled	300°		30-35	55
LAMB				
Leg	300°		30-35	40-45
Rolled Shoulder	300°		40-45	40-45
Shoulder (Bone In)	300°		30-35	40-45
VEAL				
Leg	300°		25-30	40-45
Shoulder	300°		25	40-45
Boned and Rolled	300°		40-45	40-45
PORK				
Loin	350°		35-40	50-55
Fresh Ham	350°		30-35	50-60
Smoked Pork				
Ham (New Style)	300°		15	
Ham (New Style) Half	300°		18-20	
Ham Butts	300°		35-40	
POULTRY				
Chicken				
Stuffed 3-4 pounds	350°		45-40	
Stuffed 4-5 pounds	350°		40-35	
Stuffed over 5 pounds	325°		35-30	
Turkey				
8-10 pounds	325°		25-20	
10-14 pounds	325°		20-18	
14-18 pounds	300°		18-15	
18-20 pounds	300°		15-13	
Goose				
10-12 pounds	325°		30-25	
Duck				
5-6 pounds	350°		35-30	

WORKS MAGIC
I have a special casserole
My best — without a doubt;
I merely have to mention it,
And my mate says, "Let's eat out!"

BREAKFAST CASSEROLE

Wonderful, refrigerate 12 hours before serving.

8 eggs
6 slices bread, cubed,
  remove crust
1 pound sausage,
  cooked and crumbled

2 cups milk
1 cup sharp cheddar
  cheese, grated
1 teaspoon salt
1 teaspoon dry mustard

Mix together all ingredients in bowl. Put in greased 9" x 13"
dish. Bake 35 minutes in 350° oven.

EASY SCRAMBLED EGGS

A quick way to serve eggs for several people. Bake
the large canned biscuits which is easier than toast,
serve with meat of your choice...

8 eggs
⅓ cup milk
3 tablespoons butter,
  optional

salt
pepper, optional

Break eggs into medium bowl. Add salt and milk, beat with
whisk or fork, until well mixed. If using regular skillet, melt
butter on medium high temperature, spreading over entire
skillet. Add beaten eggs and cook until soft and fluffy. I usually use a teflon pan and spray skillet with nonstick cooking
spray. Stir with teflon spatula.

PSALM 113:3
From the rising of the sun and the going down
of the same, the Lord's name is to be praised.

BREAKFAST PIZZA

Fun...easy...enjoy...

2 cans refrigerated biscuits	6 eggs
1 pound sausage	¾ cup milk
1 cup shredded mozzarella cheese	¼ teaspoon oregano, optional
1 cup shredded cheddar cheese	½ teaspoon salt
chopped vegetables of your choice: broccoli, etc.	½ teaspoon pepper
	2 cups shredded hash browns

Spread biscuits into a 9" x 12" baking dish, covering bottom and sides. Brown sausage and drain. Put sausage on pizza crust, hash browns, veggies then cheese. Beat eggs, milk, salt and pepper, then pour over sausage, potatoes and cheese. Bake for 30 minutes in 375° oven.

EGG & SAUSAGE CASSEROLE

De---licious.

12 slices white bread, crusts removed and cubed	1 jar mushrooms
	⅓ cup chopped onion
1½ pounds pork sausage	¼ cup green peppers
2 teaspoons worcestershire sauce	1 2 ounce jar pimientos, drained and chopped
6 eggs	3 cups milk
¼ teaspoon dried oregano	1 teaspoon dried mustard
½ teaspoon salt	¼ teaspoon pepper

Line a greased 9" x 13" x 2" pan with bread cubes, set aside. In a skillet, brown sausage with the onion and green pepper, drain. Stir in pimientos, sprinkle over bread. In a bowl, beat eggs, milk, worcestershire sauce, mustard, salt, pepper and oregano. Stir in mushrooms. Pour over sausage mixture. Cover and refrigerate overnight. Bake, covered, at 325° for 1 hour and 20 minutes. Uncover and bake 10 minutes longer or until a knife inserted near the center comes out clean. Let stand 10 minutes before serving.

Friendship blooms

SWEET POTATO SOUFFLÉ

Delicious for any meal!

6 sweet potatoes, cooked and mashed	⅓ cup milk
	1 teaspoon vanilla
½ cup sugar	½ cup butter
2 eggs	

Mix all ingredients until smooth and put in 8"–9" baking dish.

Topping:

⅓ cup brown sugar	2 tablespoons melted butter
2 tablespoons flour	
	⅓ cup chopped nuts

Mix all ingredients together and crumble over sweet potato mixture. Bake in 350° oven until topping is browned.

Thank you, God, for little things,
That often come our way,
The things we take for granted
But don't mention when we pray,
The unexpected courtesy,
The thoughtful kindly deed,
A hand reached out to help us
In the time of sudden need.
Oh, make us more aware, dear God,
Of little daily graces
That come to us with "sweet surprise"
From never-dreamed-of places.

Love wasn't put in your heart to stay.
Love isn't Love 'til you give it away.

CHEDDAR BAKED POTATO SLICES

Easy to make and easy to serve.

1 can mushroom soup	4 medium potatoes
½ teaspoon paprika	1 cup of cheddar cheese
½ teaspoon salt	

In small bowl, combine soup, paprika and pepper. In greased casserole dish, arrange potatoes in overlapping rows. Sprinkle with cheese and spoon mixture over cheese. Cover and bake in a 350° oven for 45 minutes. Uncover and bake for 10 more minutes. ENJOY.

JIM'S POTATOES

Easy to prepare & scrumptious.
Cook on grill or bake in oven.

Scrub potatoes. Cut into ¼" slices the amount of potatoes you are using. Place in a foil baking dish. Sprinkle lightly with seasoning salt. Add red and green sweet peppers. Add sliced onions on half of potatoes, (in case someone doesn't care for onions). Add carrots and mushrooms. Pour Italian dressing across vegetables. Adding cheese when potatoes are half done is optional, but is delicious!

FAVORITE CASSEROLE
Combine everything on the left side of refrigerator.
Add chips and bake...

OVEN CRISP POTATOES

thinly sliced potatoes   **melted butter**
seasoning salt

In shallow buttered baking pan, put layers of thinly sliced potatoes. Dribble melted butter over potatoes. Season layers with seasoning salt. Bake covered in 375° oven for 30 minutes, then uncover until brown. *(A layer of thinly sliced onions also would be good for a change.)*

GLAZED SWEET POTATOES

Easy to prepare, delicious.

4 medium sweet   **¼ cup butter**
  potatoes *or*   **¼ cup maple syrup**
2 cans sweet potatoes   **¼ teaspoon cinnamon**
⅓ cup brown sugar

Boil sweet potatoes in water, covered, only until tender. Drain, cool slightly. Peel and cut into chunks. Place cooked or canned sweet potatoes in a 2 quart baking dish. In a small saucepan, combine butter, syrup, brown sugar and cinnamon. Cook and stir until mixture boils. Pour over potatoes. Bake in a 350° oven for 25 minutes or until heated thoroughly.

ZUCCHINI CASSEROLE WITH SALSA

Tasty, easy to prepare.

thinly sliced zucchini
1 pound sausage,
cooked and drained
thinly sliced onions

1 jar salsa
sharp cheddar cheese

Layer zucchini, sausage, onions and salsa. Top with sharp cheddar cheese. Bake 30 minutes in 350° oven.

CARROT CAKE COUNTS AS A SERVING OF VEGETABLES.

SQUASH CASSEROLE

2 cups cooked squash
1 onion, finely chopped
½ pint sour cream
1 package Pepperidge
Farm dressing
2 small carrots, grated

1 can cream of
chicken soup
dash garlic salt
1 stick butter *or*
margarine

Mix dressing and one stick butter melted. Save a small amount for top. Combine remaining dressing with other ingredients and bake at 350° for 1 hour. May be frozen but do not bake if you are going to freeze.

OLD COUNTRY PROVERB
An apple a day,
keeps the doctor away,
An onion a day,
keeps everyone away.

SCALLOPED POTATOES

6 potatoes, peeled and sliced	3 tablespoons butter
1 medium onion, chopped	2 tablespoons flour
2 teaspoons salt	2 cups hot milk
pepper to taste	½ cup grated cheddar cheese

Melt butter. Add flour, salt and pepper and stir until smooth. Slowly add the hot milk, stirring constantly on medium heat. (Using wooden spatula works best.) When sauce thickens, add cheese and continue stirring until well blended. In a 1½ quart casserole that is well buttered, put layers of the sliced potatoes, onion and cheese sauce, repeating until all ingredients are used. Bake 1 hour in a 350° oven.

SUPER DELICIOUS POTATOES

That says it all!

8 medium unpeeled baking potatoes, scrubbed in length wide wedges	½ teaspoon paprika
	2 tablespoons parmesan cheese
¼ teaspoon pepper	⅓ cup oil
	½ teaspoon garlic salt

Arrange potatoes in slightly greased shallow pan. Mix remaining ingredients and swish over potatoes. Bake in preheated oven at 350° for 45 minutes or until golden brown, brushing occasionally with oil mixture. FUN, FUN.

Most folks are about as happy,
As they make up their mind to be.
A. Lincoln

I will sing of the mercies of the Lord forever!

MACARONI LOAF

1 cup cooked macaroni
2 cups scalded milk
1 cup bread crumbs
3 eggs
1 teaspoon parsley
1 tablespoon chopped
  onion

1 small jar pimento
1½ cups grated medium
  cheddar cheese
  salt *and* pepper

Grease baking dish. Whip eggs, put bread cubes in scalded milk. Combine all ingredients together in baking dish. Place dish in pan of water. Bake 50 minutes at 350°. Serve with mushroom soup over each serving.

HONEY APPLE RINGS

Great with stir fry!

½ cup honey
¼ teaspoon cinnamon
⅓ teaspoon salt
  touch of vinegar

4 medium apples,
  unpeeled, cored
  and cut into
  ½ inch rings

Combine honey, cinnamon, salt and vinegar in a large skillet, bring to boil. Add apple rings and reduce heat to simmer. Simmer for 8 minutes turning apples over once. Arrange on platter.

ASPARAGUS CASSEROLE

2 cans asparagus,
   1 pound if using fresh
2 cups crushed, seasoned
   dressing mix
⅛ teaspoon curry
8 ounces shredded
   Cheddar

½ cup chopped almonds
1 tablespoon butter
1 10½ can cream of
   chicken

If using fresh asparagus, cut in ¾ lengths. Cook in 1 cup salted boiling water until tender crisp. Drain and reserve liquid. Combine seasoned crumbs and cheese. Set aside. Combine soup, reserved liquid and asparagus. Layer half of crumb mixture in a buttered 2 quart casserole. Top with half of asparagus. Repeat with remaining ingredients. Toss chopped almonds with melted butter. Sprinkle over casserole. Bake at 350° for 30 minutes.

CARROT PUDDING

2 cups mashed carrots
1 teaspoon baking
   powder
2 tablespoons flour
1½ teaspoons cinnamon

½ stick margarine
3 eggs, beaten
¾ cup milk
1 cup sugar
½ cup brown sugar

Melt margarine in casserole. Cook carrots until soft, then cool. Mix dry ingredients. Add eggs, milk and carrots. Mix well. Add carrot mixture with butter in casserole. Bake 45 minutes to 1 hour at 325°, until crusty on top. Best with turkey, ham, etc.

COLOSSIANS 2:3, LB
In Him lie hidden all the mighty,
untapped treasures of wisdom and knowledge.

MIXED VEGETABLE CASSEROLE

1 20 ounce package mixed vegetables
1 10 *or* 20 ounce package chopped broccoli

Cheese sauce:
2 tablespoons butter *or* margarine
2 tablespoons flour
1 cup milk
1 cup Velveeta cheese

Topping:
1 16 ounce package Ritz crackers
1 stick butter *or* margarine

Cook vegetables as usual and drain. Put vegetables in 9" x 12" greased baking dish. Melt ingredients for cheese sauce over low heat. Pour sauce over vegetables. Melt stick of butter and crush crackers, mix together and sprinkle on top of cheesed vegetables. Bake in 350° oven until topping has lightly browned.

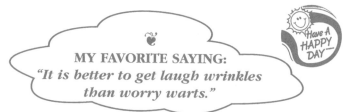

MY FAVORITE SAYING:
"It is better to get laugh wrinkles than worry warts."

Have A HAPPY DAY

BAKED ACORN SQUASH

Delicious and easily prepared for a main dish. Serve with cranberry salad or pineapple casserole.

2 medium size acorn squash
melted butter

salt and pepper
brown sugar *or* honey

Wash, cut in half and remove seeds from squash. Place upside down in baking pan with ¼" water. Bake in hot oven at 400° for 30 minutes. Turn squash over and brush lightly with melted butter or margarine. Sprinkle with salt and pepper. Add a little brown sugar or honey. Return to oven and bake 30 minutes longer or until tender.

Dishes, dishes, tools of toil,
The more you eat, the more you soil,
The more you soil, the worse you feel,
And then you're ready for another meal.

CHICKEN BROCCOLI CASSEROLE

4 to 6 chicken breasts
2 10 ounce boxes
frozen broccoli
1 can cream of
chicken soup
1 can cream of
mushroom soup

2 tablespoons
lemon juice
¼ cup mayonnaise
1 cup bread crumbs
1 cup grated sharp
cheddar cheese
¼ cup butter

Cook chicken until tender, cool and dice. Cook broccoli according to package directions and drain. Line bottom of casserole dish with broccoli and sprinkle chicken over broccoli. Mix soups, (undiluted), lemon juice and mayonnaise and pour over chicken. Sprinkle cheese over soup mixture. Put bread crumbs over the soup-coated mixture and top entire mixture with melted butter. Bake in 400° oven for 30 minutes or until browned.

MATTHEW 5:16
Let your light so shine before men,
that they may see your good works,
and glorify your Father which is in Heaven.

FORGOTTEN CHICKEN

Try serving with cranberry salad
or pineapple casserole.

1 can undiluted cream
  of celery soup
1 can undiluted cream
  of mushroom soup
1⅓ cups rice, uncooked

1 cup milk
1 3 pound fryer, cut up
1 package dry
  onion soup

Preheat oven to 350°. In a medium saucepan combine soups, rice and milk. Heat until barely warm. Spoon mixture into a lightly greased 3 quart casserole. Wash and pat chicken dry. Coat evenly with onion soup mix. Place over rice mixture in casserole. Cover and bake 1½ hours until fork-tender.

GOURMET GREEN BEAN BAKE

Put the french friend onions around the edge
for an attractive casserole.

2 cans whole *or*
  cut green beans
1 can mushroom soup
1 can drained
  mushrooms
1 can french fried
  onions

⅓ cup milk
¼ cup bean juice
  small can water
  chestnuts, optional

Drain beans. Blend soup, milk and bean juice. Mix all ingredients together, except the onions. Bake 20 minutes in preheated 350° degree oven until starts to bubble around the edge. Sprinkle onions around edge and bake 6 additional minutes or until the onions are nicely browned.

THINGS THAT MONEY CAN'T BUY:
Money can't buy friendship — friendship must be earned.
Money can't buy a clear conscience — square dealing is the
price tag. Money can't buy the glow of good health — right
living is the secret. Money can't buy happiness — happiness
is a mental attitude, and one may be as happy in a cottage as
in a mansion. Money can't buy sunsets, songs of wild birds,
and music of the wind in the trees — these are free as the
air we breathe. Money can't buy inward peace — peace is
the result of being right with God. Money can't buy character — character is what we are when we are alone with
ourselves in the dark. Money can't buy many of the most
valuable treasures life has to offer.

EASY TACO CASSEROLE

1 pound ground chuck
1 cup salsa
2 teaspoons chili
  powder
1 cup (4 ounces) colby
  cheese shredded
1 medium tomato,
  chopped
¾ cup sliced ripe olives

½ cup mayonnaise *or*
  salad dressing
2 cups crushed tortilla
  chips
1 cup (4 ounces)
  monterey jack
  cheese, shredded
2 cups shredded lettuce

In a saucepan, brown ground chuck, drain. Add salsa, mayonnaise, chili powder and olives. Mix well. In an ungreased 2
quart baking dish, layer half of the meat mixture, chip and
cheeses. Repeat layers. Bake uncovered, at 350° for 20–25
minutes. Just before serving, top with tomato and
lettuce...DELICIOUS...

Life, Love and Laughter.
What Priceless Gifts!

SCALLOPED PINEAPPLE

Great with ham or most meats!

3 eggs, well beaten
1½ cups sugar
3 cups 1" fresh
   bread cubes
½ cup grated cheese,
   optional

1 20 ounce can
   crushed pineapple,
   undrained
⅓ cup butter cut in
   1" squares

Combine all ingredients and stir well. Pour in lightly greased 10" x 8" x 2" baking dish. Bake at 325° for 1 hour. *Note: Maraschino cherries cut in half and arranged across the top is attractive.*

ESCALLOPED PINEAPPLE

Simple to prepare!

2 #2 cans pineapple
   chunks, drained,
   save juice
2 cups cheese, cubed
1½ cups sugar

5 tablespoons flour
2 teaspoons butter
½ stick butter
5 slices of bread, toasted

In buttered casserole pour in pineapple chunks and cubed cheese. In saucepan combine 1½ cups sugar and flour. Slowly add pineapple juice and cook until thickened. Add 2 teaspoons butter and pour over cheese and pineapple. In saucepan melt ½ stick butter, add toasted bread (torn in pieces) sprinkle on top of casserole. Bake 25 minutes in 350° oven.

CHICKEN CURRY STIR FRY

2 tablespoons olive oil
½ cup chopped Vidalia
  onion
4 (appx. 1 pound)
  boneless, skinless
  chicken breasts cut
  into small cubes
2 tablespoons water
1 tablespoon curry
  powder
¼ teaspoon salt
⅛ teaspoon pepper

⅓ cup chopped peanuts
2 tablespoons
  currants *or*
  raisins
1 10 ounce package
  frozen mixed
  vegetables
2 cups cooked rice
1 green *or* red bell
  pepper cut into
  strips (garnish)

Heat oil in large skillet or stir fry pan over medium-high heat. Add onion, cook and stir until onion is clear. Add chicken, water, curry powder, salt and pepper, stir and cook 6–8 minutes or until chicken is no longer pink. Add peanuts, currants, frozen vegetables; cook and stir 7–8 minutes. Serve over hot rice.

This house is clean enough to be healthy and dirty enough to be happy.

BAKED CHICKEN NOODLE DINNER
— BILL'S STYLE

Excellent meal for preparing ahead.
Serve with vegetable and salad.
How about Key Lime Pie for dessert?

6 to 8 chicken breasts,
  boneless and skinless
1 13 ounce package
  Mueller's ½" noodles
2 cans mushroom soup

½ cup water
2 tablespoons butter
2 tablespoons
  cooking oil

Place butter and oil in skillet to warm. Add chicken and partially cook on all sides. Prepare noodles only partially done. Place noodles in 9" x 13" baking dish and place chicken over noodles. Pour mushroom soup over chicken. For moistness, pour ½ cup water over all. Cover with foil and bake 45 minutes at 350°. Remove foil and bake 15 more minutes. Garnish with paprika and chopped chives.

This morning when I got up,
I had one nerve left...
and now you're getting on it.

CORN CASSEROLE

1 can cream style corn
1 can whole kernel corn
1 large onion, chopped
1 small can pimento,
  chopped
⅔ cup milk
1 egg, well beaten

1 cup cracker crumbs
1 cup grated cheese,
  sharp cheddar
¼ cup melted butter
2 teaspoons sugar
salt, pepper *and*
  red pepper to taste

Combine in order given. Mix and pour in casserole dish.
Bake 1 hour at 350°.

SPINACH CASSEROLE

1 package frozen
  spinach, cooked,
  drained and chopped
2 cups small curd
  cottage cheese
1 8 ounce carton
  sour cream

1 12 ounce grated
  cheddar cheese
1 stick melted butter
6 eggs, beaten
4 tablespoons flour
salt *and* pepper
  to taste

Combine all ingredients. Pour into a 2 quart casserole. Bake
in 350° oven about 45 minutes or until set.

*"Think of the good side...we finally found out that we
can drive twenty-three miles after the pointer hits 'E'!"*

BAKED BEANS

1 large can
  baked beans
1 medium onion,
  optional

½ cup catsup
½ cup brown sugar
¼ cup molasses

Mix all ingredients together. Pour in large casserole dish.
Bake 1 hour in 350° oven.

*Note: After 30 minutes, top with bacon slices for added
flavor.*

*Spread your arms to those with needs,
and serve with joy and zest;
fill each day with golden deeds,
and give your very best.*

CANDIED YAMS

The extra attention is worthwhile,
a tasty preparation.

2 large sweet potatoes
1 cup sugar
1½ teaspoons cinnamon
½ teaspoon ginger

½ cup water
¼ cup butter, broken
  in pieces

Boil sweet potatoes until almost tender and remove skins.
Mix sugar, cinnamon and ginger, add water. Slice the potatoes
into quarters and put them in a heavy skillet. Pour over sugar
mixture, over potatoes and dot with butter. Cook over low
heat, turning several times. Cook 20–30 minutes.

MASHED POTATO CASSEROLE

Delicious and nice to prepare ahead.
Goes well at pot luck dinners too.

8 medium potatoes	1 carton sour cream
1 8 ounce package	¼ cup butter
cream cheese	salt to taste
⅛ teaspoon garlic	
powder	

Peel and boil potatoes in salted water until done. Drain and mash. Add rest of ingredients. Put in a 2 quart casserole dish. Can be refrigerated for a couple of days or frozen. Cover and bake until heated thoroughly.

Note: If you have leftovers, cover with slices of American cheese and french fried onions, baking until the cheese melts.

*Lord, remind me
that nothing is going to happen
to me today
that you and I
can't handle together!*

BROCCOLI CASSEROLE

1 pound bag frozen	1 can mushroom soup
broccoli, cooked	1 cup rice, cooked
and drained	1 small jar Cheez Whiz

Combine all together. Place in baking dish. Bake at 350° for 25 minutes.

CHICKEN CASSEROLE

Delicious!

4 to 8 chicken breasts, skinned (deboned optional)

1 can mushroom soup
½ pint sour cream

Mix soup and sour cream together in small bowl and spread over chicken. Place in casserole dish, covering with lid. Bake at 350° for 2 hours. Grated cheese sprinkled over chicken is optional.

SALMON NOODLE CASSEROLE

At it's best for supper on a cold day.

1 tall can salmon
4 ounces noodles, cooked by package directions, drained
½ cup salad dressing
¼ cup milk

1 package frozen peas, cooked by package directions, drained
1 tablespoon chopped onion
½ teaspoon paprika

Mix all ingredients together in casserole. Bake in 350° oven for 30 minutes or until it bubbles around edge.

PSALM 34:1
I will bless the Lord at all times.
His praise shall continually be in my mouth.

PIPER'S STIR FRY

Easy to prepare, wonderful.

Stir fry small chicken strips in 2 tablespoons of oil. Add vegetables, such as broccoli, sliced onions, sliced mushrooms and green pepper, cook until crispy tender.

Mix 1½ cups chicken broth, 1 tablespoon soy sauce, 2 full tablespoons cornstarch, 2 teaspoons brown sugar, 1 teaspoon garlic powder and ¾ teaspoons ginger. Mix all in a bowl and put with chicken and vegetables. Boil 1 minute. Serve over rice.

PSALM 19:14
Let the words of my mouth and the meditation of my heart be acceptable in thy sight, oh Lord, my strength and redeemer.

ZUCCHINI PIE

Delicious. Makes crust as a quiche.
Great for a pot luck.

3 cups diced *or* sliced
unpeeled zucchini
½ cup grated parmesan
cheese
½ cup cheddar cheese
½ teaspoon salt

1 large onion
1 cup Bisquick
4 eggs, beaten
3 tablespoons parsley
½ cup salad oil
1 teaspoon pepper

Grease a 9" pie plate. Combine all ingredients. Mix until zucchini are all coated with mix. Bake in preheated 350° oven for 35-40 minutes.

TOMATO ZUCCHINI BAKE

3 medium zucchini,
thinly sliced
4 medium ripe
tomatoes
¾ cup grated parmesan
cheese, divided
2 tablespoons oil

¼ teaspoon garlic
powder
1 teaspoon dried
thyme
¼ teaspoon salt
¼ teaspoon pepper

Preheat oven to 375°. In 8" casserole dish, arrange half of zucchini slices. Top with half of tomato slices. Sprinkle with ¼ cup cheese. Top with remaining zucchini and tomato. Sprinkle garlic powder, thyme, salt and pepper over tomato. Drizzle with olive oil. Sprinkle remaining ½ cup cheese over top. Bake for 20-25 minutes.

Bloom where you are planted.

RUMP ROAST

Another favorite, easy.
Roast will brown beautifully on the outside.
This seals the juices inside the roast.
Drippings make wonderful gravy.

1 rump roast	**seasoned salt**
salt *and* **pepper**	**garlic salt**

Cover roast well with salt and pepper. Place in shallow baking pan. Cook in 300° oven uncovered; do not add water. Cooking time is approximately 25 minutes per pound.

DINNER WILL BE
READY WHEN
YOU HEAR THE
SMOKE ALARM GO OFF

SWISS STEAK — CROCK POT STYLE

A crowd pleaser.

3 pounds swiss *or*	**1 green pepper, sliced**
round steak	**2 tablespoons**
1 large onion	**shortening**
1 28 ounce can	**flour**
tomatoes	

Cut meat into serving size pieces and coat with flour. Brown meat in shortening. Place meat and other ingredients in crock pot. Cover and cook on low all day. Serve over rice (or can cook potatoes with meat...mushrooms optional too)! YUMMY!

MEATLOAF

A family favorite. Delicious.
A happy choice anytime.

1½ pounds ground chuck	1 teaspoon pepper
¾ cup oatmeal	2 eggs, beaten
1½ teaspoons salt	⅓ cup milk
1 tablespoon worcestershire sauce	½ cup catsup
	⅓ cup chopped onion *or*
	1 pouch dry onion soup

Mix all ingredients until well blended. Place in a greased baking pan or dish. Mix topping and put over meat loaf. Bake in 350° oven for 1 hour and 10 minutes. The topping adds a great flavor.

Topping:

½ cup catsup	3 tablespoons brown sugar
1 tablespoon worcestershire sauce	

Mix well.

HIPPOPOTAMUS STEW

Prepare with caution!

1 medium sized hippopotamus	2 rabbits, optional
	salt *and* pepper

Cut hippo in small bite sized pieces. This should take 2 months at least. Add enough gravy to cover, and cook for 4 weeks at 465° in large African skillet. Will serve about 2400 people. If more people are coming, the 2 rabbits may be added, although this is only when absolutely necessary as most people do not like to find hare in their stew...

SLOW COOKER POT ROAST

Delicious...simplify dinner today.

3 pound rump *or*
pot roast
6 medium potatoes,
quartered
1 can mushroom soup

½ cup water
6 carrots, cut into half
1 pouch Lipton's dry
onion mix

Flour roast and brown in small amount of oil. Or if in a hurry, omit this. Stir together in the slow cooker, the soups and water. Place meat and vegetables in slow cooker, cover with lid and cook all day...dinner is ready...serve with a nice salad.

*Do you ever have
one of those mornings
when you wake up and your go-go
is all gone-gone?*

BEEF CASSEROLE ITALIANO

1 pound lean
ground beef
8 to 10 ounces of
spaghetti sauce
2 10 ounce packages
frozen spinach
2 cups ricotta cheese
angel hair pasta

1 8 ounce package
mozzarella cheese
slices
salt *and* pepper
to taste

Brown ground beef and add any commercial spaghetti sauce, cook about 15 minutes. Stir in handful cooked angel hair pasta and place in a large casserole. Cook 2 10 ounce packages frozen spinach. Drain and cut in small pieces. Mix with 2 cups ricotta cheese. Place around the sides of the casserole. Top with 8 ounce package mozzarella cheese slices. Place in a 350° oven for about ½ hour or until casserole bubbles in center.

CROCK POT VEGETABLE BEEF SOUP

Great on a cold winter day!

¾ pound stew beef,
cut in small pieces
¼ teaspoon garlic salt
4 ribs celery, chopped
1 large onion, chopped
3 potatoes, cubed
2 cups water
2 16 ounce cans
tomatoes quartered

1 8 ounce can
tomato sauce
1 8 ounce can whole
kernel corn
1 package frozen
vegetable soup mix
2 teaspoons salt
¼ teaspoon ground
pepper

Mix all ingredients together in crock pot. Cook all day or all night.

GOO — LASH

A quick dish...kids love it!

1½ to 2 pounds
ground chuck
1½ cups catsup
1 cup tomato sauce *or*
enough to moisten
well
salt *and* pepper
to taste

12 ounces Mueller's
elbow macaroni
chopped onions,
optional
4 tablespoons
brown sugar
½ cup water
touch of garlic salt

Brown meat in skillet, salt and pepper and touch of garlic, (also, onions are optional). While meat is cooking, cook macaroni until done. Remove from stove and rinse well in colander. Add to meat with catsup, tomato sauce, brown sugar and water. Heat clear through and it is ready to serve.

Employer to employee: "Don't you do anything fast?"
Reply: "Yes, I get tired fast."

CHICKEN POT PIE

A delightful change of pace.
Very good. Takes the place of a quiche.

2 cans cream of
  potato soup
1 16 ounce can
  mixed Vegall
½ cup diced chicken
  pie crust as for pie

½ teaspoon thyme
  a little pepper
½ cup milk

Mix all together and put in pie pan lined with bottom crust. Crimp edges to seal (beaten egg spread over crust is optional). Bake in 350° oven for 50 minutes or until crust is nicely browned.

Note: To make preparing easier, buy the already made pie crusts in the cooler section at the grocery store.

TO PREPARE A DELICIOUS TURKEY

The perfect way to bake a turkey is to use a Reynolds turkey size bag, found in the section at the grocery store where you find Reynolds products. Make sure you follow directions on the box exactly as it states. Your turkey will brown beautifully and be moist and delicious. No mess...no fuss!

TO GET A FRESH START,
DO THESE EIGHT THINGS:
1. Be born again.
2. Accept God's forgiveness.
3. Freely forgive others.
4. Learn all you can from your mistakes.
5. Turn your weakness into your strong point.
*6. Accept what you cannot change, and with God's
help, turn it into something beautiful.*
7. Put the past behind you.
8. Get up and begin again.

CHUCK ROAST IN FOIL

Easy...no mess...very tasty.

1 chuck, round *or*
rump roast
½ to 1 envelope dry
onion soup mix

1 *or* 2 cans mushroom
sauce *or*
cream of mushroom
soup *or*
celery soup

Preheat oven to 325–350°. Place roast on large piece of aluminum foil, sprinkle with onion soup. Spread mushroom sauce on top. Wrap roast in foil, seal well. Bake for 20 minutes to 1 hour per pound or until done. Remove to heated platter.

TEX-MEX MEAT LOAF

Delicious.

1½ pounds lean
    ground beef
1 16 ounce can red
    kidney beans, rinsed
    and drained
1½ cups picante sauce
1 medium onion,
    chopped

1 clove garlic, minced
½ cup dry bread crumbs
2 eggs
1½ teaspoons ground
    cumin
1 teaspoon salt
2 tablespoons
    brown sugar

Combine meat, beans, 1 cup of the picante sauce, onion, garlic, bread crumbs, eggs, cumin and salt; mix well. Press into 9" x 5" loaf pan. Bake 1 hour at 350°. Pour off drippings. Combine remaining ½ cup picante sauce and brown sugar. Spread over meatloaf. Continue baking 15 minutes; remove and let stand 10 minutes. Serves 6.

"DIDN'T YOU USED TO BE IN MY SON JONATHAN'S PLAY GROUP?"

The people who tell you never to let little things worry you have never tried sleeping in the same room with a mosquito.

PERKY CHICKEN

Prepared in a jiffy.

skinless chicken pieces	3 tablespoons picante sauce
1 can mushroom soup	2 teaspoons teriakki sauce
1 can water	

Mix ingredients together, except for chicken pieces. Put some in bottom of casserole. Add chicken pieces and the rest of the sauce. Bake in 350° oven, covered. Bake until chicken is done.

CHICKEN CASSEROLE

Always tasty, quick to prepare. Serve with salad.

chicken pieces of your choice	7 ounce box Minute Rice
1 can mushroom soup	½ cup milk
1 can celery soup	1 package Lipton's Dry Onion Soup

Mix soups, milk and rice. Pour in 9" x 13" baking dish. Layer chicken pieces on top of soup mixture. Sprinkle onion soup over top. Cover with foil. Bake in oven at 275° oven for 2 hours.

POPPY CHICKEN

Delicious!

2 pounds chicken breasts
1 can chicken *or* mushroom soup
1 cup sour cream
6 tablespoons chicken broth

30 Ritz crackers
2 tablespoons poppy seed
½ stick butter *or* margarine

Boil chicken with some celery, onion and carrots. When chicken is done and cool enough to handle, remove from bone in large pieces and place in 2 quart casserole.

Note: You might need more chicken broth to make mixture juicy.

Mix soup, sour cream and chicken broth and pour over chicken in casserole. Crumble Ritz crackers in large pieces and put on top of chicken, then sprinkle poppy seed on top of crackers. Melt butter and pour on top of casserole. Bake 30 minutes in 350° oven.

KEEP...
A song in your heart
A smile in your talk
A twinkle in your eyes
A spring in your walk
A prayer on your lips
A light in your soul
A dream in your head
A friend new or old.

These are more precious than silver and gold.

AMERICAN CHOP SUEY

1 pound ground round steak	1 teaspoon salt
2 tablespoons oil pepper	1 cup onions, sliced
1 4 ounce jar mushrooms, with juice	1 cup green peppers, chopped
1 #2 can tomatoes	1 cup sliced celery
3 tablespoons soy sauce	¾ cup rice
	⅛ teaspoon pepper

Brown meat in oil. The add the rest of the ingredients. Bring to a boil, then lower temperature. Simmer for 1 hour in a covered pan.

HELLO,
You have reached
Doc Hugster's
answering machine.
I won't be in until
tomorrow. Until
then, please take
two arms, HUG
someone and call me
in the morning.

HUG

Hugging is Healthy

It helps the body's immunity system.
It keeps you healthier.
It cures depression.
It reduces stress.
It's invigorating.
It induces sleep.
It's rejuvenating.
It has no unpleasant side effects.
Hugging is nothing less than a miracle drug.
...SO, Hug someone Today!...

"The hurrier I go, the behinder I get."

QUICK 'N EASY BARBECUE CHICKEN

Outdoor flavor indoors.

1 chicken, cut up *or* choice of pieces
1 cup catsup
lemon pepper

4 tablespoons brown sugar
vinegar, to taste

Place chicken in an 8" square baking dish. Sprinkle each piece with lemon pepper. Combine all ingredients and pour over chicken. Cover. Bake 1½ hours at 250–300°.

BAKED CHICKEN OR TURKEY SALAD

A good way to use leftover turkey!

2 cups chicken *or* turkey, cooked and diced
2 cups celery, diced
1 can cream of chicken soup, *(not celery or mushroom)*

½ soup can milk
½ cup mayonnaise
1 tablespoon lemon juice
1 teaspoon salt
¼ teaspoon pepper
1 medium bag potato chips, crushed

Combine all ingredients except chips. Pour into baking dish. Top with chips and bake at 325° for 20 minutes or till bubbling; celery should still crunch a little! Good reheated.

MY CHICKEN DIVAN

Makes a delicious hardy meal...serve with salad.

4 chicken breasts,
deboned *or*
3 5 ounce cans
boned chicken
2 10 ounce packages
frozen broccoli *or*
1 large bunch fresh
broccoli
1 can cream of
celery soup

1 can cream of
chicken soup
1 cup mayonnaise
1 teaspoon lemon juice
½ teaspoon curry
powder
1 cup cheddar cheese,
shredded
½ cup bread crumbs
3 cups rice, cooked

Pre-cook chicken and broccoli separately. Spread broccoli in
a casserole. Place chicken on top. In separate bowl, combine
soup, mayonnaise, lemon juice, and curry powder. Pour over
chicken and broccoli. Sprinkle cheese and bread crumbs on
top. Bake at 350° for 25 minutes. Serve over cooked rice.

CHICKEN CASSEROLE

Place 2½ to 3 pound chicken kettle, (use chicken parts if you
prefer). Cook until tender. Cut chicken into bite size chunks.
Heat oven to 400°. Combine chicken with the following:

2 cups chopped celery
1 small can black olives
2 tablespoons
grated onion
1 cup mayonnaise
½ cup chopped
toasted peanuts

salt to taste
4 tablespoons
lemon juice
1 cup crushed potato
chips for topping

Pile lightly in casserole or individual dishes. Sprinkle with ½
cup grated cheese and 1 cup crushed potato chips. Bake 20
minutes for casserole, less for individual servings.

REDNECK FRIED CHICKEN

A traveling salesman was driving down a dirt road when a weird looking chicken ran in front of his car, he jammed on the brakes after stopping he looked around and saw the chicken running up the driveway, backing up he drove up to the house. Said to the farmer outside that sure is a funny looking chicken! Sure is said the farmer, you see there are three of us, me, my wife and son, we always fight over the drum sticks, so I made some changes in genes of the eggs and came up with a six legged chicken so we wouldn't have to fight over them. How do they taste asked the salesman? Don't know said the farmer, can't catch one.

CURRY — CAJUN SPICED CHICKEN

Good Cajun eating.

⅓ cup honey
1 tablespoon water
3 tablespoons dijon mustard
2 tablespoons margarine, melted
1½ teaspoons cajun seasoning

1 teaspoon curry powder
1 teaspoon lemon juice
1 clove garlic, minced
6 skinless, boneless chicken breast halves

In 9" x 13" baking dish combine honey, water, mustard, margarine, cajun seasoning, curry powder, lemon juice and garlic; mix well. Add chicken breast halves, turning to coat. Arrange in a single layer. Bake uncovered, in a 350° oven for about 30 minutes or until chicken is tender and no longer pink. Serve chicken and pan drippings over spinach pasta or hot cooked rice.

LONG & SHORT

A city fellow stopped his car near a farmstead and asked the farmer how far it was to Poughkeepsie.

"Well," said the farmer, taking off his hat and scratching his head, "if you continue the way you're headed, I'd say it's about 25,000 miles. But if you turn around and head the other way, it's 7 miles."

CHICKEN TETRAZZINI

A very good dish.

1 8 ounce package elbow macaroni
3 cups cubed cooked chicken
1 can peas, drained
1 package onion soup mix

¼ cup pimento
½ cup green pepper
2 cups shredded cheese
¼ cup almonds, optional

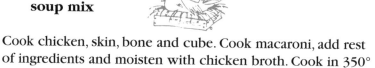

Cook chicken, skin, bone and cube. Cook macaroni, add rest of ingredients and moisten with chicken broth. Cook in 350° oven until heated through and bubbly.

PINEAPPLE GLAZED CHICKEN

Easy...do ahead.

2 cups pineapple tidbits
¼ cup pineapple juice
2 tablespoons chopped fresh parsley
4 whole chicken breasts, halved and skinned

½ cup pineapple preserves
2 tablespoons vegetable oil
1 teaspoon cumin
½ teaspoon salt

Combine all ingredients, except chicken breasts, and blend. Place chicken breasts in glass baking dish. Pour marinade over chicken and chill, covered, for at least 30 minutes. Broil or grill 6" from heat, until browned, 8-10 minutes, turning once.

HAWAIIAN CHICKEN

Everyone will want this recipe.

1 chicken *or*
favorite pieces
½ cup brown sugar
½ cup soy sauce
¼ teaspoon ginger
1 tablespoon vinegar

½ cup pineapple juice
2 tablespoons
cornstarch
½ stick butter *or*
margarine

Coat pieces of chicken with butter or margarine. Bake 45 minutes in 325° oven. Blend rest of ingredients and pour over chicken. Put pineapple pieces on top. Juice will get thick. Cover with foil this time and cook another hour in 325° oven.

TODAY IS THE DAY

Today is the day for creating, rejoicing, singing, praising,
forgiving, and enjoying.
Today is the day for enriching, blessing, praying, observing,
standing, and advancing.
Today is the day for learning, adventuring, laughing,
befriending, thanking, and touching.
Today is the day for encouraging, healing, sharing, listening,
thinking, and planning.
Today is the day for growing, dreaming, searching,
discerning, meditating, and persisting.
Today is the day for choosing, loving, trusting, caring,
empathizing, and giving.
Today is the day for playing, preparing, daring, inspiring,
attempting, and producing.
Today is the day for focusing, cooperating, studying, working,
selling, and improving.
Today is your day. What will you do with it?

MUSTARD TARRAGON CHICKEN

Marinade:
- 1 8 ounce sour cream
- ⅓ cup Dijon mustard
- 1 teaspoon dried tarragon
- 2 tablespoons sugar
- ½ teaspoon salt
- 2 tablespoons lemon juice
- pinch pepper

Chicken:
- 3 whole chicken breasts, skinned and halved
- ¾ cup dry bread crumbs
- 3 tablespoons margarine, melted

Combine marinade ingredients in a bowl. Add chicken to mixture coating each piece completely. Cover bowl and refrigerate overnight. Heat oven to 350°. Lightly grease 13" x 9" baking dish. Remove chicken from marinade. Arrange in single layer in baking dish and spoon remaining marinade over chicken. In a small bowl, combine bread crumbs and margarine. Spoon evenly over chicken. Bake uncovered at 350° for 55-60 minutes or until chicken is tender and juices run clear. Serve over rice. Serves 6.

A good laugh and a long sleep
are the two best cures.

WALDORF ASTORIA STEW

Nice on a winter day.

3 pounds lean beef,
cut into 1" cubes
2 medium onions,
chopped
2 cups carrots,
cut in small pieces
1 cup celery, sliced

4 medium potatoes,
peeled and cut
into chunks
2 teaspoons salt
dash pepper
3 tablespoons tapioca
4 cups tomato juice

Cook in slow cooker all day or medium oven for 4 hours.

*Recall it as often as you wish,
a happy memory never wears out.*

BAR-B-Q RIBS

Do ahead and refrigerate.

Use own judgement on amount of ribs to use for this sauce.

Simmer for ½ hour:

2 medium onions,
sliced thin
1 clove garlic
1 cup catsup

2 tablespoons
worcestershire sauce
1 cup water
¼ cup brown sugar

Brown ribs. Pour off fat. Cover with above sauce. Bake 2 hours at 350°. Works out well if done in crock pot also. Sauce can also be used to pour over chicken.

Note: You might want to boil ribs and drain off fat.

SWEET & SOUR PORK

1 pound lean pork cubed
¼ teaspoon salt
1 cup water
1 cup diced celery
½ cup diced onion
1 #1 can mushrooms

1 #2 can crushed pineapple
3 tablespoons sugar
1 tablespoon cornstarch
3 tablespoons vinegar
1 tablespoon soy sauce
4 tablespoons butter *or* margarine

Cook pork with salt in water until white; drain. Combine celery, onion and mushrooms; cook in 2 tablespoons butter for 5 minutes. Add pineapple, bring to boil. Combine sugar, cornstarch, vinegar and soy sauce; add to pineapple mixture. Cook until thickened. Melt remaining butter in skillet; add pork. Cook for 5 minutes, stirring constantly. Pour pineapple mixture over pork; cover. Bake at 350° for 45 minutes. Serve with rice or baked potato, if desired.

PSALM 34:4
*I sought the lord and he answered me;
and he delivered me from all my fears.*

HAM & BROCCOLI HOT DISH

Easy main course dish.

1 package noodles
1 package frozen
  broccoli, thawed
1 can ham, cut in pieces
1 jar Cheez Whiz

1 stick butter
1 onion, chopped
1 can cream of
  mushroom soup,
  low sodium/low fat

Melt butter, add onions, mushroom soup and Cheez Whiz. Cook noodles until tender, drain. Add noodles to the above, add ham and broccoli. Bake in large pan at 325° for 1 hour.

LOVE WASN'T
PUT IN YOUR
HEART TO
STAY LOVE
ISN'T LOVE
'TIL YOU
GIVE IT
AWAY

HAM & MACARONI CASSEROLE

Different for a change!

½ pound macaroni
2 tablespoons butter
1 tablespoon
   minced onion
1 tablespoon flour
½ teaspoon dry mustard
½ teaspoon salt
2 teaspoons paprika
   dash of pepper

2 cups milk
1½ cups chopped
   cooked ham
2 cups grated
   cheddar cheese
¾ cup fresh
   bread crumbs
2 tablespoons
   melted butter

Cook macaroni according to package and drain. Melt butter in double boiler. Add onions, flour, salt, pepper and paprika. Stir in milk gradually and cook over boiling water until smooth and thickened. Add ham and 1½ cups cheese; cook, stirring constantly until cheese is melted. Put macaroni in greased 2 quart casserole dish. Pour ham sauce over it. Toss lightly with fork until macaroni is coated. Sprinkle remaining cheese over top. Mix melted butter with bread crumbs, sprinkle over cheese. Bake in preheated oven at 400° for 20 minutes.

Two choices for dinner:
Take it or leave it.

Life is easier than you think —
All you have to do is:
Accept the impossible,
Do without the indispensable,
Bear the intolerable and
Be able to smile at anything.

GREG'S BAKED SPAGHETTI

Spaghetti the easy way and good too!

2 **pounds ground chuck**
1 **large jar of chunky**
   Prego sauce

1 **large package**
   spaghetti
   mozzarella cheese

Brown meat. Add Prego sauce. Line baking dishes, such as a small glass pie pan or with a generous portion of spaghetti. Add spaghetti sauce over spaghetti. Cover with mozzarella cheese. Bake in 350° oven until the cheese is melted. Serve with toasted french bread.

A pilot was in Hong Kong and met a fellow who claimed he had been a Kamikaze pilot in World War II and he said that his name was Chow Mein. The U.S. pilot said Kamikaze pilots were suicide pilots and if he had really been a Kamikaze pilot he would probably have been dead by now. He said, "Well, just call me Chicken Chow Mein..."

Smile, God loves you.

SHRIMP CREOLE

A colorful main dish,
pink shrimp and green pea pods.

2 tablespoons butter
2 medium onions, chopped
1½ teaspoon salt
¼ teaspoon pepper
1 tablespoon flour
2 cups cooked shrimp
1 pint frozen snow peas, partially defrosted

½ medium green pepper, chopped
½ cup celery, chopped
1 large can tomatoes
⅛ teaspoon red pepper
1 cup water
1 teaspoon sugar
2 teaspoons creole seasoning

Melt butter in skillet. Saute green pepper, onions and celery until tender. Add tomatoes, salt, pepper, red pepper and water. Cover and cook about 10 minutes. Combine flour and sugar; add enough water to make a smooth paste and stir into tomato mixture. Cook and stir until slightly thickened. Add shrimp and pea pods; cook until pea pods are tender, about 5 minutes. Serve with fluffy rice.

JOHN 1:12
But as many as received him,
to them gave he power to become
the Son of God,
even to them that believe on his name.

Anything that takes me two hours to cook...
should take you more than two minutes to eat!

MEXICALI CHICKEN

2 skinless split chicken breasts	1 small can mushrooms, chopped
1 can mushroom soup	½ cup brown rice
1 can Rotel's diced tomatoes & chilis	½ cup water

Put chicken breasts in casserole. Mix remaining ingredients. Pour over chicken breasts. Cover and bake at 350° for 1¼-1½ hours.

II PETER 3:9
The Lord is not slack concerning his promise,
as some men count slackness;
but is longsuffering toward us,
not willing that any should perish,
but that all should come to repentance.

The Seven Ages of the Married Cold

1st Year Cold

The husband said, "Sugar dumpling. I'm really worried about my baby girl! You've got a bad sniffle and there's no telling about these things with all the strep going around. I'm putting you in the hospital this afternoon for a general check-up and a good rest. I know the food is lousy there, so I'll be bringing you food from Tosini's. I've already got it all arranged with the floor superintendent."

2nd Year Cold

"Listen, darling. I don't like the sound of that cough! I've called Dr. Miller to rush over here. Now you go to bed like a good little girl just for Poppa."

3rd Year Cold

"Maybe you better lie down, Honey. Nothing like a little rest when you feel lousy. I'll bring you something. Do you have any canned soup?"

4th Year Cold

"Now look dear, be sensible! After you've fed the kids, washed the dishes and finished vacuuming, you'd better lie down."

5th Year Cold

"Why don't you take a couple of aspirin?"

6th Year Cold

"If you'd just gargle or something. Instead of sitting around barking like a dog!"

7th Year Cold

"For Pete's sake, stop sneezing! Are you trying to give me pneumonia!?"

Desserts

SUBSTITUTIONS

FOR...	YOU CAN USE...
1 tablespoon cornstarch	2 tablespoons flour *or*
	1½ tablespoons quick cooking tapioca
1 cup cake flour	1 cup less 2 tablespoons all-purpose flour
1 cup all-purpose flour	1 cup plus 2 tablespoons cake flour
1 square chocolate	3 tablespoons cocoa and 1 tablespoon fat
1 cup melted shortening	1 cup salad oil
	(may not be substituted for solid shortening)
1 cup milk	½ cup evaporated milk and ½ cup water
1 cup sour milk *or* buttermilk	1 tablespoon lemon juice *or* vinegar and enough sweet milk to measure 1 cup
1 cup heavy cream	⅔ cup milk and ⅓ cup butter
1 cup heavy cream, whipped	⅔ cup well-chilled evaporated milk, whipped
sweetened condensed milk	No substitution
1 egg	2 tablespoons dried whole egg and 2 tablespoons water
1 teaspoon baking powder	¼ teaspoon baking soda and 1 teaspoon cream of tartar *or* ¼ teaspoon baking soda and ½ cup sour milk, buttermilk *or* molasses; reduce other liquid ½ cup
1 cup sugar	1 cup honey; reduce other liquid ¼ cup; reduce baking temperature 25°
1 cup miniature marshmallows	About 10 large marshmallows cut-up
1 medium onion (2½" diameter)	2 tablespoons instant minced onion *or* 1 teaspoon onion powder *or* 2 teaspoons onion salt; reduce salt 1 teaspoon
1 garlic clove	⅛ teaspoon garlic powder *or* ¼ teaspoon garlic salt; reduce salt ⅛ teaspoon
1 tablespoon fresh herbs	1 teaspoon dried herbs *or* ¼ teaspoon powdered herbs *or* ½ teaspoon herb salt; reduce salt ¼ teaspoon

THE BAKER'S LAMENT
Why is it that when I'm alone
And choose to bake a cake,
The whole thing comes out wonderful,
Without the least mistake?
But when I've guests to entertain,
There's no sense to deny it;
Like the tower of Pisa, my poor cake
Is totally lop-sided!

CARROT CAKE

Tried and True.

2 cups sugar	2 teaspoons baking powder
4 eggs	2 teaspoons cinnamon
1⅓ cups cooking oil	4 cups carrots, grated
2 cups flour, sifted	¾ cup nuts, chopped
2 teaspoons baking soda	cream cheese frosting

Preheat oven to 350°. Grease and flour 13" x 9" baking pan. If using glass pan, oven should be at 325°. This cake may also be baked as layer cake, using two 9" pans.

Blend eggs, oil and sugar well. Sift flour, baking soda, baking powder and cinnamon. Pour into the egg and oil mixture. Blend until flour is just incorporated, a few seconds. Scrape down. Place mixture in a bowl and fold in carrots and nuts. Spoon batter into pan; bake in oven for 35–40 minutes. Cool cake. If freezing, do not frost until ready to use.

CREAM CHEESE FROSTING

1 8 ounce package cream cheese	1 teaspoon vanilla
½ cup margarine	1 pound confectioners' sugar

With metal blade in place, blend ingredients until smooth and velvety. Frost cake.

COCONUT LAYER CAKE

A delicious cake for any occasion,
also great for a wedding cake!

Cake:
- ½ cup butter *or* margarine, softened
- ½ cup shortening
- 2 cups sugar
- 5 eggs, separated
- 2 cups all-purpose flour
- 1 teaspoon baking soda
- 1 cup buttermilk
- 2 teaspoons vanilla extract
- 2 cups flaked coconut
- ½ cup chopped pecans

Frosting:
- 1 8 ounce package cream cheese, softened
- 4 cups (1 pound) confectioners' sugar
- ¼ cup butter *or* margarine, softened
- 1 teaspoon vanilla extract
- ¼ cup flaked coconut, toasted
- pecan halves

In a large mixing bowl, cream the butter, shortening and sugar until light and fluffy. Add egg yolks and beat well. Combine flour and baking soda; add to creamed mixture alternately with buttermilk. Stir in vanilla. Add coconut and pecans. In a small mixing bowl, beat egg whites until stiff; gently fold into batter. Pour into two greased and floured 9" round cake pans. Bake at 350° for 40 minutes or until a wooden pick inserted near the center comes out clean. Cool 10 minutes in pans before removing to wire racks; cool completely. For frosting, beat cream cheese, sugar, butter and vanilla until smooth and creamy. Spread between layers and over top and sides of cake. Sprinkle with coconut; garnish with pecans. Yield: 12–16 servings.

Greg and Patty's Wedding Cake

RED VELVET CAKE

A delicious, beautiful holiday cake!

½ cup shortening
1½ cups sugar
2 eggs, beaten
2 cups flour
3 tablespoons cocoa
½ teaspoon salt

1 cup buttermilk
1 ounce red food
   coloring
1 teaspoon baking soda
1 tablespoon vinegar

Cream shortening and sugar and add eggs. Sift flour, cocoa, and salt together, and mix buttermilk with coloring. Add dry ingredients alternately with liquid ingredients to creamed mixture. Beat well. Dissolve baking soda in vinegar and fold into batter. Grease and flour two 9" layer-cake pans. Bake at 350° for 30–35 minutes. Remove from pans, cool, and spread with vanilla filling and frosting (see below).

VANILLA FILLING & FROSTING

Sometimes I double this recipe.

¼ cup flour
1 cup milk
⅛ teaspoon salt
½ cup shortening

½ cup softened butter
1 cup sugar
1 tablespoon vanilla
   coconut, optional

In a small saucepan, blend flour with milk and salt and cook over low heat, stirring, until of pudding consistency. Cool. In large mixer bowl cream together shortening, butter, sugar, and vanilla. Add cooled pudding mixture and beat until smooth. Spread between layers and over top and sides of cake. Sprinkle coconut on top if desired. Refrigerate cake.

THE VALUE OF A SMILE

It costs nothing, but creates much. It enriches those who receive without making those who give poor. It happens in a flash and the memory sometimes lasts forever. None are so rich they can get along without it and none so poor but are much richer for a smile. It creates happiness in the home, fosters good will in business and is the counter sign of friendship. Yet it cannot be bought, begged, borrowed or stolen, for it is something that is no earthly good to anybody till it is given away. And if it ever happens that someone should be too tired to give you a smile, why not give them yours? For nobody needs a smile so much as those who have none left to give.

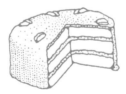

NAN'S CHOCOLATE POUND CAKE

1 box german chocolate cake mix *or*
regular chocolate cake mix

Instead of recipe on back of box use only:
1 cup water   3 eggs
⅓ cup vegetable oil

Separate 3 extra eggs and beat the egg whites until stiff. Fold gently into batter. Pour into well greased tube pan and bake at 350° about 25 minutes. Check with toothpick coming out clean. Cool about 20 minutes. Either frost or serve plain.

ZUCCHINI CAKE

Easy and delicious!

3 eggs, beaten
1 cup salad oil
2 cups sugar
2 cups zucchini,
  unpeeled and grated
3 teaspoons cinnamon
1 teaspoon salt

1 teaspoon soda
½ teaspoon
  baking powder
3 cups flour
1 cup walnuts,
  chopped

Beat eggs until lemon colored. Add salad oil, sugar, zucchini, cinnamon, salt, soda, and baking power. Mix well and gradually add flour and walnuts. Put into a greased 3-quart Bundt pan. Bake at 350° for 1 hour.

PSALM 107:8,9
Let them give thanks to the Lord
for his unfailing love
and his wonderful deed for men,
for he satisfies the thirsty
and fills the hungry with good things.

STRAWBERRY CAKE

Pretty cake if made in a Bundt pan.

Cake:

1 package Pillsbury white cake mix
1 small box frozen strawberries *or*
1 pint fresh berries, pureed, reserve 2 tablespoons

1 3 ounce package strawberry Jello
4 eggs, unbeaten
¾ cup Wesson oil
1 teaspoon vanilla

Mix all ingredients and pour into a greased Bundt pan. Bake for 1 hour at 350°. Cool.

Icing:

1 stick butter
2 tablespoons strawberries

1 box powdered sugar

MAKE A JOYFUL NOISE!

ORANGE COFFEE CAKE

A superb cake.

Cake:

1 Duncan Hines orange cake mix	4 eggs
1 3 ounce package instant vanilla pudding	1 teaspoon vanilla
	1 teaspoon butter flavoring
⅔ cup orange juice	½ cup sugar
¾ cup Wesson oil	2 teaspoons cinnamon
	½ cup pecans, chopped

Mix ½ cup sugar, cinnamon and pecans together. Set aside. Beat all other ingredients together at high speed until nicely blended. Pour ⅓ batter into greased and floured tube pan or two 9" cake pans. Sprinkle some of the filler on top of batter. Add more batter, more filler until it is all used. Bake for 1 hour at 350°. Cool 8 minutes in pan. Pour glaze over cake.

Glaze:

1 cup powdered sugar	orange juice, pulp from orange is good
½ teaspoon vanilla	

Mix together sugar, orange juice and vanilla. Add enough orange juice to make glaze consistency. Pour over cake. This may be frozen and used at a later date.

BEST-EVER POUND CAKE

A good cake for any occasion!

3½ cups flour
1½ teaspoons
   baking powder
3 cups sugar
1 stick margarine

1 cup shortening
5 eggs
1 teaspoon vanilla
1 teaspoon lemon juice
1 cup milk

Preheat oven to 325°. Sift dry ingredients together. Cream sugar, margarine and shortening. Add eggs, one at a time, beating after each. Add vanilla and lemon juice. Add milk and flour alternately. Mix well. Bake at 325° for 1 hour and 30 minutes. *Do not open oven for 1 hour!*

OREO COOKIE DESSERT

Prepare ahead. Easy and tasty!

1 regular package
   oreo cookies,
   crumbled
1 gallon vanilla
   ice cream, softened

⅓ cup melted butter
1 can fudge topping
   maraschino cherries,
   optional

Mix cookies with butter. Press half in a 9" x 13" pan. Freeze... cover mixture with topping, cover topping with softened ice cream. Sprinkle with remaining crumbs and return to freezer. Garnish with cherries before serving if desired.

Capture all the joys of life!

A way to know you have had a bad day:
When you come home from work and rip the
"HAVE A HAPPY DAY" bumper sticker off your car...

CHERRY CHEESECAKES

Makes a hit at pot lucks!

24 vanilla wafers
2 8 ounce packages
   cream cheese, softened
¾ cup sugar
2 eggs

1 tablespoon
   lemon juice
1 teaspoon vanilla
1 22 ounce can
   cherry pie filling
   Cool Whip

Place paper liners in 24 muffin cups and put one vanilla wafer in each. Combine cheese, sugar, eggs, lemon juice and vanilla. Beat until smooth and creamy. Fill muffin cups about two-thirds full. Bake at 350° for 15–20 minutes. Cool thoroughly. Spoon cherry pie filling on top with a dollop of Cool Whip or whipped cream if desired. Refrigerate until ready to serve.

Enjoy the cherries
Endure the pits...

SHORTCUT
SOUR CREAM COFFEE CAKE

Easy, marvelous for a brunch. Stores well.

Cake:

1 box yellow cake mix	4 eggs
1 8 ounce carton	3 tablespoons
sour cream	brown sugar
¾ cup salad oil	2 teaspoons cinnamon
½ cup sugar	1 cup pecans, chopped
1 teaspoon vanilla	

Mix first five ingredients in a bowl. Combine remaining
ingredients for filling in separate bowl. Grease and flour tube
or Bundt pan. Pour half of the batter into pan. Sprinkle one-
half of the filling over batter. Repeat. Bake at 350° for 1 hour.

Glaze:

1 cup powdered sugar	3 tablespoons milk

Combine sugar and milk, pour over warm cake.

BANANA CAKE

Always good for a change of pace.

2 cups all-purpose flour	2 eggs
1 teaspoon soda	2 medium size bananas,
¼ teaspoon salt	mashed
½ teaspoon cinnamon	¼ cup buttermilk
¾ cup shortening	1 teaspoon vanilla
1½ cups sugar	

Heat oven to 350°. Grease two 9" cake pans. Sift flour with
soda, salt and cinnamon. Cream shortening, add sugar gradually, add one egg at a time, beating after each addition. Add
mashed bananas to buttermilk and add alternately with flour
beginning and ending with flour. Add vanilla. After mixing
thoroughly, turn into prepared pans. Bake 30–35 minutes.
Cool in pans a few minutes then turn on racks to cool.

*Did you hear about the person who thought
a balanced diet was a hamburger in both hands?*

COKE CAKE

This could make you famous!

2 cups flour   2 cups sugar
1 teaspoon   1 teaspoon soda
  baking powder

Mix the above and set aside.

2 sticks butter   2 tablespoons cocoa
1 cup Coke

Bring the above to a boil and beat with the first mixture.
Add ½ cup buttermilk, 2 eggs, 1 tablespoon vanilla and 1 cup
miniature marshmallows. Mix with other mixture and bake
in a preheated 350° oven for 30-35 minutes.

Icing:
Bring to a boil 1 stick butter, ¼ cup Coke plus 2 tablespoons,
and 3 tablespoons cocoa. Remove from stove and add 3 cups
sifted powdered sugar and 1 teaspoon vanilla.

CARAMEL ICING

Great on chocolate, banana or most any cake!

3 cups sugar   2 sticks butter *or*
½ cup milk   margarine

Mix all together in a heavy pan and bring to a boil. Start tim-
ing and boil hard for 3 minutes. Remove from heat and add
a pinch of soda and 1 teaspoon vanilla. Beat with electric
mixer until smooth and creamy. If it gets to hard, add a touch
of milk to soften. Spread on cooled cake.

DANISH COFFEE CAKE

The buttermilk makes the difference.
Do ahead and freeze! Serves 18.

2¼ cups sifted flour
1 tablespoon cinnamon
1 tablespoon nutmeg
½ teaspoon salt
¾ cup sugar
1 cup brown sugar,
firmly packed

¾ cup salad oil
1 egg
1 cup buttermilk
1 teaspoon baking soda
½ cup pecans, chopped
1 teaspoon vanilla

In a mixing bowl, combine the first seven ingredients.
Reserve ½ cup for topping. Add egg. Blend. Add buttermilk
mixed with soda and blend all ingredients well. Pour mixture
into a greased and floured 9" x 13" pan. Sprinkle with ½ cup
of topping and press it in with a spoon. Preparation time: 20
minutes. Bake: 30-35 minutes.

🍒 THINKING ABOUT THE CROSS 🍒

It reminds me to be thankful
For my blessings every Day,
To strive to serve him better
In all I do and say.

It's also a daily reminder
Of the peace and comfort I share,
With all who know my Master
And give themselves to his care.

So when I think about the cross,
It should daily remind me,
That Jesus is the Lord of my life,
If I always let him be.....

7 MINUTE ICING

A favorite, very easy to make.

¾ cup sugar	3 egg whites
dash salt	7 tablespoons
1 teaspoon vanilla	white corn syrup

Bring water to boil in a double boiler pan. Water should touch bottom of pan inserted in water. Put all ingredients in pan and beat together with hand mixer for 7 minutes or until stiff peaks form. Do not overbeat. Icing should not loose gloss. Spread quickly on cake. You'll be so happy you tried this. Let it be a fun experience for people to druel over.

SHEET CAKE

Another favorite!

Cake:

2 cups flour	4 tablespoons cocoa
1 teaspoon soda	1 cup water
2 cups sugar	½ cup buttermilk
½ cup margarine	2 eggs
½ cup salad oil	2 teaspoons vanilla
½ teaspoon cinnamon, optional	

Mix flour, soda and sugar together. Bring margarine, salad oil, cocoa and water to boil, pour over dry ingredients. Mix well. Add butter, eggs and vanilla. Mix well. Pour into greased 11" x 17" x 1" cookie sheet or jelly roll pan. Bake at 375° for 20 minutes or until done. (Some ovens vary, use the toothpick test.)

Icing:

Melt ½ cup margarine (1 stick), 4 tablespoons cocoa and 6 tablespoons buttermilk together and boil for only 1 minute. Remove from stove and add 1 box confectioners' sugar and vanilla and mix well. Add 1¼ cups chopped nuts and ice cake while it is hot...YUMMY!

You know you have had a bad day
when you write your frustrations out in M & M's
and eat them one paragraph at a time...

MIRACLE CHEESE CAKE

Delicious...

1 package lemon flavored gelatin	1 teaspoon vanilla
1 cup boiling water	1 tall can Milnot, whipped
3 tablespoons lemon juice	3 cups graham cracker crumbs
1 8 ounce cream cheese	½ cup butter *or*
1 cup sugar	margarine, melted

Dissolve gelatin in boiling water. Add lemon juice. Cool.
Cream together cheese, sugar and vanilla. Add gelatin. Mix
well. Fold whipped Milnot into gelatin mixture. Crush graham crackers into fine crumbs and add melted butter. Pack
two-thirds of mixture in bottom of 9" x 13" pan. Add filling
and sprinkle with remaining crumbs. Chill. Delicious!

Laughter is contagious. Start an epidemic!

PEANUT BUTTER PIE

Easy, delicious.

4 ounces cream cheese
1 cup powdered sugar
⅓ cup peanut butter
½ cup Carnation Milk *or* Milnot

1 8 ounce carton Cool Whip
¼ cup chopped salted peanuts

Beat cream cheese until light and fluffy. Add powdered sugar then peanut butter. Slowly add milk. Fold in Cool Whip. Turn into 9" graham cracker crust. Sprinkle ¼ cup nuts over top. Cover and freeze until ready to serve.

MIRACLE COBBLER

Melt one stick of butter or margarine in a medium casserole dish.

Mix:
1 cup self rising flour
1 cup sugar

1 cup milk

Pour over melted margarine or butter, pour in 16 ounce can of sweetened fruit, your choice (sliced peaches, apples or cherries). Bake for 1 hour at 350°.

I Wish I Was A Teddy Bear
❶ Everybody likes 'em
❷ Nobody cares how fat they are
❸ The older they get, the more they're worth

A friend joyfully sings with you
when you are on the mountain top.
And silently walks beside you
when you are in the valley.

PERFECT NEVER FAIL PIE CRUST

Rolls out wonderful.

2 cups flour
1 teaspoon salt
1 cup Crisco

6 to 7 tablespoons
ice water

Mix flour, salt and Crisco together with pastry blender until crumbled very well. Add ice water and mix with fork only until pie dough holds shape. Put half of pie dough on a floured surface and roll out to desired size.

BUTTERSCOTCH PIE

A recipe you'll enjoy either with
whipped cream or meringue.

6 tablespoons butter
1 cup brown sugar
2 tablespoons flour
1⅔ cups milk
1 teaspoon vanilla

1 cup boiling water
3 tablespoons
corn starch
½ teaspoon salt
3 egg yolks

Melt butter in pan until golden brown. Add brown sugar and boil until foamy, stirring constantly. Stir in the water. Remove from heat. In another pan, mix the cornstarch, flour, salt and milk. Stir gradually until smooth. Stir in the brown sugar mixture and cook over medium heat until mixture boils. Boil 1 full minute. Remove from heat and stir a cup of mixture into egg yolks, slightly beaten. Then blend into hot mixture. Boil 1 minute longer. Pour into baked pie shell. If using whipped cream, chill pie and keep refrigerated. YUMMY!

Have you heard about the rotation diet? Every time you turn around you are eating...

CUSTARD PIE

4 eggs slightly beaten	½ teaspoon
½ cup sugar	almond extract
¼ teaspoon salt	2½ cups scalded milk
½ teaspoon vanilla	nutmeg

Blend eggs, sugar, salt, vanilla and almond extract. Gradually stir in scalded milk. Pour into pie shell. Bake in hot oven 25-30 minutes. Pie is done when knife inserted halfway between outside and center comes out clean. Remove and sprinkle with nutmeg.

CUSTARD BREAD PUDDING

3 cups milk	pinch of salt
2 cups bread crumbs	nutmeg
¼ cup raisins	cinnamon
½ cup sugar	1 teaspoon vanilla
3 eggs	
4 tablespoons melted butter	

Preheat oven to 350°. Scald milk. Then add bread crumbs and well beaten eggs. Stir and add rest of ingredients. Bake slowly 30-45 minutes in oven.

COCONUT PIE

Melts in your mouth!

2 cups milk,
  reserve ¼ cup
¼ cup cornstarch
3 egg yolks
½ cup sugar

¼ cup white syrup
1 teaspoon vanilla
¼ teaspoon
  coconut flakes

Heat milk. Meanwhile, place cornstarch, egg yolks, ½ cup
sugar, white syrup and ¼ cup of milk in a bowl. Beat well,
add to the milk that is heating and stir with wooden spatula
until mixture thickens and cook while stirring 1 more
minute. Add flavorings and coconut. Stir. Pour into baked
pie shell. Top with meringue.

3rd JOHN 2
*Beloved, I wish above all things that you prosper
and be in health, even as thy soul prospereth.*

*I will sing
of the mercies of the Lord
forever!*

DELICIOUS BANANA PUDDING

Excellent!

1¼ cups sugar	4 tablespoons butter
3 cups milk	3 eggs, separated
⅓ cup plain flour	2 teaspoons vanilla

Mix sugar and flour together. Slowly blend in the milk. Beat egg yolks well and stir into other ingredients, preferably with wire whisk. Cook over medium heat until bubbly and thick. Stir in butter and vanilla, stirring constantly, cooking while stirring for 1 more minute. Layer crumbled vanilla wafers, bananas and pudding in that order. Can sprinkle wafer crumbs lightly over top *or*

Make meringue:
Mix 3 egg whites with ¼ teaspoon cream of tartar, and 6 tablespoons sugar on high until shiny. Spread on pudding and bake in 350° oven until meringue is light brown.

PECAN PIE

So easy. Absolutely perfect and absolutely delicious!

3 eggs
½ stick butter
dash salt
1 cup pecans

1 cup white syrup
½ cup sugar
1 teaspoon vanilla
1 pie crust

Lightly beat eggs, stir in the rest of the ingredients and pour into pie crust. Bake in preheated 350° oven and bake for 45-50 minutes on lower rack in the oven, to keep the pecans from getting too brown.

EASY CHOCOLATE PIE

Delicious!

2 sticks margarine
4 eggs, mix sugar
with eggs
1 cup sugar

1 cup chocolate chips
1 cup nuts
1 cup coconut

Melt chips and margarine. Blend in sugar, eggs, nuts and coconut. Pour into 2 unbaked pie shells. Bake at 350° for 30-35 minutes.

MARK 11:23–24

*For verily I say unto you, that whosoever
shall say unto this mountain,
be thou removed, and be thou cast into the sea:
and shall not doubt in his heart,
but shall believe that those things which he saith
shall come to pass: he shall have whatsoever
he saith. Therefore I say unto you,
what things soever you desire, when you pray,
believe that you receive them,
and you shall have them.*

Love
Laughter
Friendship
Are always welcome at our house!

BANANA SPLIT PIE

Delicious...

Crust:
2 packages   4 tablespoons
  graham crackers   powdered sugar
1 stick butter, melted

Mix, press in pan, bake at 375° for 8 minutes.

Filling:
2 sticks butter, melted   2 eggs
2 cups powdered sugar

Mix and beat for 15 minutes. Add sliced bananas, sliced strawberries, drained crushed pineapple; fold into the filling and spread over crust. For a topping, spread whipped cream over top and add nuts.

Note: Store bought graham crackers or butter crust can be used.

KEY LIME PIE

Easy as pie, gorgeous, delicious too!

2 eggs, separated
1 15 ounce can
  sweetened condensed
  milk
½ teaspoon vanilla
2 to 3 drops green
  food coloring

1 8" graham cracker
  pie shell
½ cup lime juice
3 tablespoons sugar

Beat egg yolks and mix thoroughly with milk. Fold in lime juice and food coloring. Pour into pie crust. Beat egg whites a few seconds and add sugar. Beat until stiff. Spread over pie and put under broiler until lightly browned, or can be browned in 350° oven for 8-10 minutes. Refrigerate 3-4 hours before serving.

This house is protected by a thick layer of dust. Please do not remove.

Have A HAPPY DAY

LEMON PIE

1 graham cracker crust
½ cup lemon juice
1 teaspoon grated
  lemon rind
1 can condensed milk

2 eggs, separated
¼ teaspoon cream
  of tartar
4 tablespoons of sugar

Combine lemon juice and rind slowly. Add milk and eggs yolks and stir until well blended. Pour into chilled crust. Add cream of tartar to egg whites and sugar. Beat until it holds a firm peak. Put meringue on pie and brown in a 350° oven.

CHERRY BREEZE

*Prepared in a breeze! Nice summer dessert.
No bake crust...no cook filling!*

1 cup crushed vanilla
wafers
⅓ cup butter, melted
1 8 ounce package cream
cheese, softened
1 15 ounce can
sweetened condensed
milk

½ cup lemon juice
1 teaspoon vanilla
1 21 ounce can chilled
cherry pie filling

Mix crumbs and butter well in 9" pan. Press firmly and evenly over bottom and sides of pan to form crust. Chill. Beat cream cheese until light and fluffy. Add condensed milk and mix well. Stir in lemon juice and vanilla. Pour into crust. Refrigerate 3-4 hours or until firm. Just before serving, top with chilled pie filling.

PUMPKIN PIE CRUNCH

1 package yellow
cake mix
1 16 ounce can
pumpkin
1 12 ounce can
evaporated milk
3 eggs

1½ cup sugar
4 teaspoons pumpkin
pie spice
½ teaspoon salt
1 cup chopped pecans
1 cup butter, melted

Preheat oven to 350°. Grease bottom of 13" x 9" x 2" pan. Combine pumpkin, milk, eggs, sugar, spices and salt in large bowl. Mix well. Pour into pan. Sprinkle dry cake mix evenly over pumpkin mixture, top with pecans. Drizzle with melted butter and bake for 50-55 minutes or until golden brown. I have best luck by cooking on bottom rack in oven. Delicious hot or cold! Serves 16-20.

CRANBERRY APPLE CRISP

Great!

2 cups fresh uncooked
  cranberries

3 cups diced
  fresh apples
¾ cup sugar

Put above in casserole dish.

Topping:

1 stick margarine,
  melted
1¼ cups uncooked
  quick oatmeal

⅓ cup plus 1 tablespoon
  flour
½ cup nuts, chopped
½ cup brown sugar

Mix together and crumble across casserole dish. Cook 1 hour in 350° oven or until top is browned.

*When we spread sunshine in the lives of others,
we're warmed by it ourselves.*

APPLE SLICES

8 cups sliced apples
2½ cups sugar
  melted butter

1 cup crushed
  corn flakes
3 teaspoons cinnamon

Roll out pie crust to fit cookie sheet extending dough over sides. Sprinkle crushed cornflakes over dough. In large bowl, mix the apples, sugar and cinnamon together. Place over pie dough. Dribble melted margarine over apples, then put a top crust over apples and seal like pie crust. Beat egg whites until foamy and spread on top of crust. Bake at 350° for 45 minutes or until crust is light brown. While hot, frost with mixture of powdered sugar and lemon juice or regular powdered sugar icing. Cut into squares. Freezes well.

LEMON MERINGUE PIE

9" baked pie shell

Filling:

⅓ cup cornstarch,
heaping
1½ cups sugar
¼ teaspoon salt
1½ cups water
4 egg yolks, slightly
beaten

⅓ cup lemon juice
2 tablespoons grated
lemon peel, optional
2 tablespoons butter *or*
margarine

Meringue:

4 egg whites (½ cup),
at room temperature

¼ teaspoon cream
of tartar
½ cup sugar

Preheat oven to 400°. In a small saucepan, combine cornstarch, sugar and salt. Gradually add 1½ cups water, stirring until smooth. Over medium heat, bring to boiling, stirring constantly; boil 1 minute, stirring. Remove from heat; quickly stir half of hot mixture into egg yolks, mixing well. Return to saucepan, blending well. Over medium heat, return to boiling, stirring; boil 1 minute. Remove from heat. Stir in lemon juice, lemon peel, and butter. Pour immediately into pie shell. Meanwhile, preheat oven. Make meringue in a medium bowl, with a portable electric mixer at medium speed, beat egg whites with cream of tartar until soft peaks form when beater is raised. Gradually beat in sugar, 2 tablespoons at a time, beating well after each addition. Continue to beat until stiff peaks form when beater is raised. Spread meringue over hot filling, carefully sealing to edge of crust. Bake 7–9 minutes, or just until meringue is golden. Let cool on wire rack, away from drafts, at least 1 hour before serving.

Seen on
Grocery Store Bulletin Board:

FOR SALE:
Full set of Britannica
Encyclopedias!
Excellent condition.
No longer needed.
Wife knows
everything!

BUTTERSCOTCH ICEBOX COOKIES

These are sure to please!

6 cups flour, sifted	1 cup brown sugar
1 teaspoon baking soda	2 eggs
½ teaspoon salt	½ teaspoon maple
1 cup butter	flavoring
1 cup sugar	

Mama Nuck never gave us the instructions on her recipes, so
here's how I do it: Sift dry ingredients together and set aside.
Cream sugar, brown sugar, and butter. Add eggs and vanilla
and beat well. Add dry ingredients a cup at a time. Mixture
will be very stiff so put away the utensils and use your
hands! Put in 5 rolls in waxed paper, and refrigerate for several hours. When ready to bake, slice very thin, ¼", and bake
on ungreased cookie sheet in a 375° oven for 12 minutes. If
you want to get fancy, top each cookie with a pecan half
before baking. Dough will keep 3 weeks in refrigerator,
longer in freezer.

SOFT MOLASSES COOKIES

A great cookie and great for Ginger Bread cookies.

2 teaspoons baking soda
2 tablespoons hot water
½ cup shortening
½ cup granulated sugar
½ cup molasses
1 egg
2¼ cups flour

1 teaspoon ginger
1 teaspoon cinnamon
¼ teaspoon salt
6 tablespoons
   cold coffee or water
½ cup raisins

Preheat oven to 400°. Dissolve soda in hot water. Stir well and set mixture aside to cool. Work shortening and sugar until fluffy, add molasses. Stir in unbeaten egg, and beat well. Sift flour, ginger, cinnamon, and salt, and add with coffee/water to shortening mixture. Stir in soda mixture and raisins. Bake for 12 minutes.

The Perfect Man

He's quiet.
He's sweet.
And if he gives you any guff,
You can bite his head off.

CINDY'S SLICE SUGAR COOKIES

1 cup sugar	1 cup butter
1 egg	1 tablespoon vanilla
2¼ cups flour	1 teaspoon soda
additional sugar	

Mix: Sugar and butter. Beat in egg and vanilla until light and fluffy. Mix in flour and soda. Divide dough into halves. Shape each into a roll about 1½" in diameter. Wrap and refrigerate one hour. Cut into ¼" slices. Place on ungreased baking sheet and sprinkle generously with additional sugar. Bake at 375° for 10–12 minutes or until lightly browned on edges. Cool on a rack.

STRESSED IS DESSERTS SPELLED BACKWARDS!

SOUTHERN PECAN BARS

Crust:

1 box yellow cake mix	1 egg
½ cup margarine, melted	

Combine 3 cups of cake mix with melted margarine and egg until mixed. Press evenly into greased 13" x 9" x 2" pyrex dish. Bake at 350° for 20 minutes or until golden brown.

Filling:

3 eggs	1¼ cups pecans
½ cup brown sugar, packed	1½ cup dark corn syrup
	1½ teaspoons vanilla

Beat eggs and brown sugar. Add remaining cake mix, syrup and vanilla. Beat 1 minute. Pour over hot crust and sprinkle with nuts. Bake at 350° for 35 minutes or until filling sets. Cut with hot, wet knife. Makes forty-eight 2" x 1" bars.

BLESSINGS
Cookies in the oven,
Grandkids at the door.
I'm a twice-blessed woman,
Who could ask for more!

SOUR CREAM COOKIES

The old-fashioned kind, with raisins.

2 cups sugar	½ teaspoon salt
1 cup butter	1 teaspoon nutmeg
2 eggs	1 cup sour cream
3 cups flour	1½ cups raisins
1 teaspoon baking soda	1 teaspoon vanilla

Cream sugar and butter together. Add eggs and beat well. Sift together dry ingredients and add alternately with sour cream to creamed mixture. Add raisins. Drop by teaspoonsful on cookie sheet and bake at 375° for 7 minutes. Makes 5 dozen.

PSALM 119:103
How sweet are your words to my taste,
sweeter than honey to my mouth!

A fellow had just completed taking parachute lessons and had jumped out of the airplane. His parachute didn't open and as he was going down, he met someone coming up. He yelled, "Hey, do you know anything about parachutes?" And the reply came, "No, do you know anything about gas stoves?"

THUMB COOKIES

A dainty and altogether fetching confection.
Keep them small.

1 cup butter
½ cup sugar
2 egg yolks, beaten
½ teaspoon vanilla
1½ cups flour

pinch salt
raspberry *or*
apricot jam
½ teaspoon cinnamon

Cream butter and sugar. Add egg yolks and vanilla and beat well. Mix in flour and salt. Form into balls just big enough to hold a thumbprint. Place on ungreased cookie sheet 1½" apart. Press thumb into center of each cookie to make an indentation. Fill indentation with dab (about ¼ teaspoon) of jam. Bake in 350° oven for about 15 minutes. They should still be very pale when cooked. Makes about 40.

SUGAR COOKIES

The butter makes the difference.

2 cups sugar
1 cup butter
2 tablespoons
   buttermilk
1 teaspoon vanilla

5 cups flour
3 eggs
1 teaspoon
   baking soda

Mix all ingredients well. Chill dough well or overnight. Roll out on pastry cloth to ⅛" thickness. Cut in desired shapes. Bake at 400° for 7-8 minutes.

Note: Depending on the weather, a little more flour might be necessary for dough to roll out easily. Use spatula to put on cookie sheet and also to remove...have fun!

COCONUT COOKIES

1 cup butter
1 cup brown sugar
½ cup chopped nuts
1 teaspoon soda
1 teaspoon salt
2 cups coconut

1 cup white sugar
2 eggs
2 cups flour
½ teaspoon
   baking powder
2 cups Wheaties

Mix butter and the sugars together. Add eggs and mix very well. Stir in rest of ingredients. Form into 1" balls. Bake in 350-375° oven for 12-15 minutes.

Today, this kitchen is closed. This chicks had it...

CHEWY CHOCOLATE CHIP COOKIES

1 cup butter, softened
1¼ cup firmly packed
    brown sugar
½ cup white sugar
2 teaspoons vanilla
1 teaspoon baking soda
2½ cups quick oatmeal

2 eggs
2 tablespoons milk
1¾ cups flour
½ teaspoon salt
1 12 ounce package
    chocolate chips

Beat butter and sugars together until creamy. Add eggs, milk and vanilla; beating well. Add dry ingredients and mix well. Add vanilla and chocolate chips and mix well. Drop by rounded tablespoons on ungreased cookie sheet. Bake in preheated 350° oven for 9-10 minutes. Cool 1 minute on cookie sheet, then remove to wire rack or waxed paper.

 Thinking of you

THESE GOODIES SAY "I LOVE YOU"
...when mailed to someone away from home.
Necessities: Toothpaste — Deodorant — Hair gel/spray — Pencils — Stamps — Laundry Soap — Aftershave — Toothbrush — Sock or Pantihose — Gloves — Batteries — Shampoo — Disposable Razors —
                                    Money.
Foods: Trail Mix — Tea Bags — Gourmet Coffee — Cup of Soup Packages — Beef Jerky — Crackers — Cookies (Homemade) — Fudge — Pudding Cups — Microwave Popcorn — Chewing Gum — Breath Mints —Hot Cocoa Mix —
    Money.
Fun: Set of Jacks — Water Pistol — Exercise Video — Music Tape or CD — Jigsaw Puzzle — Hair Accessories — Balloons — Nerf Ball — Poster — Rubber Stamps — Cartoon Book — T-Shirt —
        Flowers AND Money!

Have a happy day!

SPECIAL K BARS

Easy & quick. Children enjoy these.

1 cup white syrup	7 cups Special K cereal
1 cup sugar	1 cup peanut butter
1¼ cups butterscotch bits	½ cup chocolate chips

Bring syrup and sugar to a rolling boil. Remove promptly from burner. Stir in peanut butter and mix well. Pour over the 7 cups of Special K cereal and stir until well mixed. Press lightly into a greased 9" x 13" pan. Melt the chips in a double boiler. When melted, mix together and spread over cereal... eat to your hearts content.

JOHN 3:3
Verily, verily, I say unto thee,
"Except a man be born again,
he cannot see the Kingdom of God."

Tourist: A person who travels a thousand miles to get a picture of himself standing by his car!

FORGOTTEN COOKIES

A great cookie for a Ladies Tea!

2 eggs whites	1 cup chopped pecans
⅔ cup sugar	1 cup chocolate chips
dash of salt	1 teaspoon vanilla

Preheat oven to 350°. Beat egg whites until foamy, gradually adding sugar. Continue beating until stiff. Add salt, pecans, chips and vanilla. Mix well and drop by teaspoon on foil. Place cookies in oven. Immediately turn off heat and leave in closed oven overnight.

BROWNIES

Absolutely delicious.
Chocolate lovers can't resist these!

2½ sticks butter	2 cups sugar
¾ cup cocoa	1 cup flour
1 teaspoon baking powder	½ teaspoon salt
1 teaspoon vanilla	4 eggs

Melt butter, add cocoa and sugar, mixing together. Beat in eggs. Add flour, salt, baking powder and vanilla. Put in a greased 9" x 13" pan. Bake in a 350° oven for 20 minutes.

TOFFEE

2 cups sugar　　　　**½ cup water**

Boil the above to a rolling boil. Add 3 sticks of butter (do not use margarine). Stir constantly, cooking to 310° on a candy thermometer. Pour on buttered cookie sheet. Spread thin. Melt 1 pound sweet chocolate in double boiler. Spread over candy. Top with finely ground nuts if desired.

HARD CANDY

Fun to make, nice for gifts. I use cinnamon oil and red food coloring, and wintergreen oil with green food coloring for the holidays.

2 cups sugar　　　　**1 teaspoon candy**
1 cup water　　　　　　　**flavoring oil**
¾ cup light corn syrup　**½ teaspoon food color**
　　　　　　　　　　　　powdered sugar

First, prepare 2 large cookies sheets by buttering and covering with ¼" powdered sugar. Make rows in sugar lengthwise with your finger about 1" apart. Combine sugar, water and corn syrup in heavy saucepan. Cook, stirring constantly, until sugar is dissolved. Then cook to 300° without stirring. Quickly remove from heat, stir in flavoring and food coloring, and pour into the rows you made in the cookie sheets. As soon as candy is cool enough to touch and barely begins to harden, cut with scissors into bite-size pieces. Allow to cool thoroughly and store in airtight container. This can also be used to make suckers. For thick candy use 1 cookie sheet.

Bloom where you are planted.

PEANUT BRITTLE

Easy and fun to make.

2 cups sugar	1 cup white syrup
½ cup water	2 teaspoons soda
2 teaspoons butter	2 cups raw peanuts
1 teaspoon vanilla	

Bring water to boil, add sugar and syrup. Cook on medium heat and stir lightly until mixture has mixed well and is clear in color. Continue to cook without stirring until mixture is very light brown in color. Add peanuts and cook until mixture spins a thread from spoon. Remove from stove and add the vanilla, butter and soda. Stir quickly and pour on buttered cookie sheets, or buttered Reynolds wrap. When cool lift with knife and break into pieces...absolutely wonderful if done correctly.

SPICED PECANS

1 cup sugar	1 cup water
1 teaspoon cinnamon	¼ teaspoon cinnamon
¼ teaspoon salt	1 teaspoon vanilla
2½ cups whole pecans	

Combine all ingredients except vanilla and pecans in saucepan. Cook over medium heat to 232° on candy thermometer or thread stage. Remove from heat. Add vanilla and pecans, stirring until nuts are well coated and mixture is creamy. Pour onto greased platter or baking sheet. Separate nuts with spoons or forks while cooling.

One of life's mysteries is how a two-pound box of candy can make a woman gain five pounds.

NEVER FAIL FUDGE

¾ cup evaporated
   skim milk

2 cups sugar
3 tablespoons butter

Melt and bring the above to a boil. Boil hard for 2 minutes. Remove from stove and add 12 ounces semi-sweet chocolate chips, 1 teaspoon vanilla and 1½ cups chopped pecans. Spread in buttered 9" square pan.

DIVINITY

2½ cups sugar
   ¼ teaspoon salt
   2 egg whites

½ cup light corn syrup
½ cup water
1 teaspoon vanilla

Combine sugar, syrup, salt and water into a saucepan. Stir only until sugar dissolves. Cook over high heat until mixture reaches 260° on a candy thermometer. Remove from heat, cool for 3-4 minutes. Meanwhile, beat egg whites to stiff peaks. Gradually pour syrup over egg whites in a thin stream, beating at high speed with electric mixer. Add vanilla and beat until candy holds its shape and starts to lose its gloss. Quickly drop from a teaspoon onto waxed paper. Part of the candy can be tinted with a touch of red or green cake coloring. Store in airtight containers.

JUST FOR FUN

Laughing is the Best Medicine!

Murphy joined the airforce and making his very first jump, the instructor told him when he jumped out of the plane to say "Geronimo" and pull the cord. A few days later, Murphy woke up in the hospital and asked, "What was the name of that Indian?"

A person had sent their picture into the Lonely Hearts Club and it was returned saying, "We're not that lonely."

A son had lost his father, and a friend asked the son, "Son, did your father have any last words?" The son answered, "No, mother was with him until the end."

A fellow was bragging about his new hearing aid to a friend, about how great it was, that he could hear everything, that he wished he had gotten it along time ago, that it was simply wonderful, that he didn't have any problems anymore. His friend asked him what kind it was and he looked at the watch on his arm and said, "Twenty after two."

One summer day a 79 year old woman who was proud that she didn't think she looked old for her age, went into the drugstore and, talking about the heat, said to the clerk, "Going to be ninety-seven today." The man reached across the counter, shook her hand and said, "Happy Birthday!" The lady took to her bed for a week...

Low Fat

WHEN YOU

Need Approximate Measurements

1 lemon makes 3 tablespoons juice
1 lemon makes 1 teaspoon grated peel
1 orange makes ⅓ cup juice
1 orange makes about 2 teaspoons grated peel
1 chopped onion, medium makes ½ cup pieces
1 pound unshelled walnuts make 1½ to 1¾ cups shelled
1 pound unshelled almonds makes ¾ to 1 cup shelled
8 to 10 egg whites make 1 cup
12 to 14 egg yolks make 1 cup
1 pound shredded American cheese makes 4 cups
¼ pound crumbled blue cheese makes 1 cup
1 cup unwhipped cream makes 2 cups whipped
4 ounces (1 to 1¼ cups) uncooked macaroni
makes 2¼ cups cooked
7 ounces spaghetti makes 4 cups cooked
4 ounces (1½ to 2) uncooked noodles makes 2 cups cooked

DAILY EXERCISE
FOR THE NON-ATHLETIC

Making the rounds is a calorie guide citing a recent medical association report: "Proper weight control and physical fitness cannot be attained by dieting alone. Many people who are engaged in sedentary occupations do not realize that calories can be burned by the hundreds, by engaging in strenuous activities that do not require physical exercise."

Here's the guide to calorie-burning activities
and the number of calories per hour they consume:

Beating around the bush	75
Jumping to conclusions	100
Climbing the walls	150
Swallowing your pride	50
Passing the buck	25
Throwing your weight around (depending on your weight)	50-300
Dragging your heels	100
Pushing your luck	250
Making mountains out of molehills	500
Hitting the nail on the head	50
Wading through paperwork	300
Bending over backwards	75
Jumping on the bandwagon	200
Balancing the books	25
Running around in circles	300
Eating crow	225
Tooting your own horn	25
Climbing the ladder of success	750
Pulling out all the stops	75
Adding fuel to the fire	150
Wrapping it up at the day's end	12
Pulling someone's leg	125
Cutting corners	50
Walking a fine line	25
Skating on thin ice	400
Making ends meet	700
Wrestling with your conscious	600
Turning over a new leaf	75
Jumping in with both feet	150
Spilling the beans	25
Blowing an exam	75
Cleaning up your act	250
Throwing in the towel	30
Taking the bull by the horns	400
Burying the hatchet	100
Turning the tables	250
Shooting off your mouth	125
Splitting hairs	25
Raising cain	225

Every time I get the urge to exercise, I just lay down until the urge leaves.

CRISPY CHICKEN STICKS

Very good...low fat...easy to prepare.

2 skinless, boneless medium chicken breasts
1 tablespoon parmesan cheese

⅓ cup cornflake crumbs
3 cups corn meal
nonstick spray coating

Rinse chicken; pat dry with paper towels. Cut chicken into pieces about 2" strips. In a shallow bowl combine cornflake crumbs, cornmeal, parmesan cheese and paprika. Lightly salt each piece of chicken. Dip each chicken piece in flour, then in a little water. Roll in cornmeal mixture to coat. Spray a baking sheet with nonstick coating. Place chicken on the baking sheet. Bake in a 375° oven for 20-25 minutes or until tender and no longer pink.

This house is under a scientific research for household dust. Do not disturb.

OVEN CHICKEN

Another good choice.

Sprinkle lemon pepper and Lawry's seasoning salt over chicken pieces. Broil in oven for approximately 10 minutes on both sides until done, or place in a covered casserole with a little water to cover bottom of casserole. Bake in 325° oven or until tender. It is best to partially skin chicken.

MUSTARD TARRAGON CHICKEN

Marinade:
- 1 8 ounce sour scream
- ⅓ cup Dijon mustard
- 1 teaspoon dried tarragon
- 2 tablespoons sugar
- ½ teaspoon salt
- 2 tablespoons lemon juice pinch pepper

Chicken:
- 3 whole chicken breasts, skinned and halved
- ¾ cup dry bread crumbs
- 3 tablespoons margarine, melted

Combine marinade ingredients. Add chicken to mixture coating each piece completely. Cover bowl and refrigerate overnight. Heat oven to 350°. Lightly grease 13" x 9" baking dish. Remove chicken from marinade. Arrange in single layer in baking dish and spoon remaining marinade over chicken. In a small bowl, combine bread crumbs and margarine. Spoon evenly over chicken. Bake uncovered at 350° for 55-60 minutes or until chicken is tender and juices run clear. Serve over rice. Serves 6.

MOTORCYCLE
COWASOCKY

Just a reminder that we are all udderly flawed !

CHICKEN & FRUIT SALAD POCKETS

Salad Mixture:
- 3 cups chopped, cooked chicken breast
- ¾ cup seedless grapes, cut in half
- ½ cup chopped celery
- ½ cup slivered almonds, toasted
- 1 11 ounce can mandarin orange segments, drained

Salad dressing:
- 2½ teaspoons sugar
- ½ teaspoon seasoned salt
- ¼ teaspoon black pepper
- ½ cup low-fat plain yogurt
- ½ cup light mayonnaise
- 1 tablespoon vinegar
- 6 wheat bread pockets

Combine chicken, grapes, celery, almonds and oranges. Mix sugar, salt, pepper, yogurt, mayonnaise and vinegar for dressing. Pour dressing over salad mixture; toss gently. Serve in wheat bread pockets. Serves 6.

Guess what I lost this week...

© 1997 Barbara Johnson.

My glasses.

One exercise program has you doing entire routines while cleaning house. It sounded so simple to bend over my vacuum cleaner and extend my right leg straight behind me, while I touched my head to my knee. That was just before the vacuum sucked up my nightgown, causing me to nearly pass out.

CURRIED BROCCOLI & ROTINI

3 ounces rotini *or* gemelli pasta, (1⅓ cups)
1 tablespoon olive oil *or* cooking oil
1 teaspoon curry powder
3 cups broccoli flowerets
½ cup chopped red *or* green sweet pepper

½ cup plain low-fat yogurt
⅓ cup reduced-sodium chicken broth
4 teaspoons all-purpose flour
1 teaspoon prepared mustard
dash salt
1 jar mushrooms

Cook pasta according to package directions, except omit salt. Meanwhile, in a large skillet heat oil. Add curry powder and stir-fry over medium-high heat for 1 minute. Add broccoli and sweet pepper; stir-fry for 3–4 minutes or till crisp-tender.

For sauce, in a small saucepan, stir together the yogurt, chicken broth, flour, mustard and salt. Stir into broccoli mixture. Cook and stir till thickened and bubbly. Cook and stir for 1 minute more. Add pasta to broccoli mixture; toss to mix. Heat through. Serve immediately. Makes 4 servings.

TURKEY GOULASH

1 to 1½ pounds   1 8 ounce package
   ground turkey   elbow macaroni
1 medium onion   ⅓ cup water
1 14 ounce bottle catsup,   3 tablespoons sugar
   (or more to taste)

Boil macaroni while browning turkey and onion together.
Drain macaroni, adding to turkey mixture. Add catsup, sugar
and water to mixture and mix well. Heat thoroughly and
serve. (Lean ground chuck also my be used.)

*A lady said she was allergic to sweets
because they made her break out in fat.*

SALAD SANDWICH

Layer thin slices of tomato, onions, cucumbers, green pepper,
mushrooms and etc. on 2 slices of firm bread or toast. Spread
lightly with salad dressing or mayonnaise of your choice.
Some days you might want to use sliced turkey on the sand-
wich or swiss cheese. Oh yes, sprinkle seasoned salt on part
of the vegetables! YUM YUM! *Then pray that it doesn't fall
apart. Ha!*

I LEARNED THAT FIBER
IS VERY IMPORTANT
FOR YOUR DIET.

SO THIS MORNING
I ATE A WICKER CHAIR.

PARMESAN TURKEY PATTIES

1 **pound fresh ground turkey**	2 **tablespoons grated parmesan cheese**
1 **teaspoon seasoned salt**	3 **tablespoons catsup**
½ **teaspoon crushed oregano**	2 **tablespoon dry bread crumbs**
	1 **tablespoon margarine**

Combine all ingredients except margarine, shape into four patties. Melt margarine in skillet. Pan fry patties in margarine about 5 minutes, or until brown; turn and brown the other side. Yields 4 patties.

A person took up horseback riding to lose weight.
They didn't lose any weight,
but the horse lost 20 pounds.

LOW FAT ITALIAN TURKEY SPAGHETTI (Diabetic)

½ cup chopped onion
½ pound lean
   ground turkey
1 8 ounce can
   tomato paste
1⅓ cups water
2½ teaspoons Italian
   seasoning
½ teaspoon
   onion powder

½ teaspoon
   garlic powder
¼ teaspoon oregano
⅛ teaspoon pepper
1 bay leaf
1 cup chopped fresh *or*
   canned tomatoes
2 cups cooked spaghetti

In large skillet, cook onion and ground turkey over medium heat until turkey is brown. Drain off any fat that accumulates. Add tomato paste, water, spices and tomatoes; mix thoroughly. Simmer mixture for at least 1 hour, adding more water if needed. Yields 4 servings. Serve ½ cup sauce over ½ cup cooked spaghetti.

Yes, I believe in angels,
and I'm sure that you do, too,
And I'm convinced that angels
are watching over you.

CRUNCHY OVEN FRIED FISH

Very good. Squeeze a little lemon juice over it.

1 pound fresh or frozen orange roughy *or* other white fish fillets, 1/2" thick
1/4 cup all-purpose flour
1/4 teaspoon salt
1/4 teaspoon lemon pepper
1 egg white

1/4 cup fine dry bread crumbs
1/4 cup cornmeal
1½ teaspoons finely shredded lemon peel
1/2 teaspoon dried basil, crushed
1/2 teaspoon paprika

Thaw fish, if frozen. Cut into serving-size pieces. In a shallow dish combine flour, salt, lemon pepper and paprika; set aside. Beat egg white until frothy. Combine bread crumbs, cornmeal, lemon peel, and basil. Dip top of fish fillets into flour mixture, shaking off any excess. Then dip into egg white, then coat with bread crumb mixture.

Spray a shallow baking pan with nonstick spray coating. Place fillets in baking pan coating side up, tucking under any thin edges. Bake in a 450° oven for 6–12 minutes or until fish flakes easily with a fork. Makes 4 servings.

WHAT TO DO
IN CASE OF EMERGENCY
1. Pick up your hat.
2. Grab your coat.
3. Leave your worries on the doorstep.
4. Direct your feet to the sunny side of the street.

HALIBUT STEAKS

Delicious!

halibut steaks   **Italian dressing**
lemon pepper

Sprinkle fish generously with lemon pepper. Marinade in Italian dressing. You can grill, bake or broil. Turn over when brown on one side. Fish is done when flakes easily. Cooking time depends on thickness of fish.

SALMON PATTIES

1 15½ ounce can salmon,   ½ cup milk
   drained   16 to 20 crushed crackers
2 eggs beaten

Mix thoroughly and shape into patties. Spray skillet with Pam and brown on both sides on medium heat. Makes 4 patties.

CREATE IN ME A
CLEAN HEART, OH GOD

AND RENEW A **RIGHT SPIRIT**
WITHIN ME.
PSALM 51:11

"I love peanuts, but I refuse to eat them,"
said the woman to her friend.
"Why is that?" asked her friend. "Have you ever seen
a skinny elephant?", the woman replied.

DELUXE CARROT CAKE (Diabetic)

4 eggs	2¼ teaspoons cinnamon
½ cup vegetable oil	1½ cups packed,
1 cup unsweet pineapple	grated carrot
juice concentrate	2½ cups all-purpose flour
¼ cup unsweet orange	2½ teaspoons baking soda
juice concentrate	1 teaspoon vanilla

Preheat oven to 325°. Grease and flour a 13" x 9" x 2" baking pan. In large bowl, combine eggs, oil and concentrates. Beat mixture until foamy on medium speed of electric mixer. Add cinnamon, carrots and flour; stir by hand until mixed thoroughly. Add baking soda; stir quickly to mix. Immediately pour batter into prepared pan. Bake 30–35 minutes. Cool on wire rack. Spread with cream cheese frosting.

CREAM CHEESE FROSTING

1 3 ounce package	1 cup fructose
cream cheese, softened	1 teaspoon
¼ cup reduced calorie	vanilla extract
margarine, softened	

In small bowl, cream together cheese and margarine until smooth. Slowly add sweetener, mix until smooth. Stir in vanilla and mix thoroughly. Spread over cooled cake.

Climb every mountain,
Ford every stream,
Follow every rainbow--
That oughta help
Slim down those thighs

PUMPKIN BARS (Diabetic)

½ cup margarine,
softened
½ cup apple juice
concentrate
¼ cup granulated
fructose
½ cup mashed banana,
(one medium banana)
1 egg
½ cup canned pumpkin

2 teaspoons vanilla
1½ cups all-purpose flour
2 teaspoons cinnamon
1 teaspoon ginger
1 teaspoon allspice
1 teaspoon baking soda
½ cup raisins
½ cup chopped pecans
vegetable cooking
spray

Preheat oven to 325°. With electric mixer, combine margarine, apple juice concentrate, fructose and mashed banana. Beat in egg, pumpkin and vanilla. Stir flour, cinnamon, ginger, allspice, and baking soda in a medium bowl until blended. Stir dry ingredients into pumpkin mixture. Add raisins and nuts. Spread into 9" x 13" pan which has been sprayed with nonstick vegetable coating. Bake for 25 minutes or until firm in center.

Dieting would be easier
if celery tasted more like chocolate cake!

ISAIAH 26:3
Thou wilt keep him in perfect peace
whose mind is stayed on thee.

A new Chinese diet —
eat all you can, but use only one chopstick.

OAT BRAN MUFFINS

Another variant on a common theme these days.

2¼ cups oat bran
¼ cup raisins *or*
   chopped dates *or*
   chopped dried apricots
¼ cup brown sugar
1 tablespoon
   baking powder

1¼ cups skim milk
2 egg whites
2 tablespoons olive oil
1 teaspoon cinnamon
½ teaspoon pumpkin
   pie spice
1 teaspoon vanilla

Combine all ingredients. Spoon mixture into muffin tins
which have been sprayed with pan spray or use paper liners.
Bake at 425° for 15-17 minutes.

YOGURT DIP

½ cup each non-fat
   yogurt, peeled and
   diced cucumber *and*
   minced celery

½ teaspoon
   garlic powder
3 teaspoons chopped
   green onion

I'm on such a strict diet that I'm not even allowed
to play dinner music!

LOW CHOLESTEROL
OATMEAL COOKIES

½ cup brown sugar
½ cup white sugar
½ cup Puritan oil
1¼ cups oatmeal
½ cup nuts
2 egg whites

½ teaspoon cinnamon
½ teaspoon
  baking powder
3 tablespoons skim milk
½ cup white raisins
1 teaspoon vanilla

Mix all together and bake at 375° for 8-10 minutes.

Help! I can't see the scale!
I ate a ton of sugar
It made me very sweet
It also made me very round —
now I can't find my feet.

LEMON
ZUCCHINI BREAD (Diabetic)

⅓ cup unsweetened apple sauce
⅔ cup apple juice concentrate
⅓ cup fructose
⅓ cup oil
2 eggs
1 tablespoon lemon juice
1 teaspoon vanilla
1 teaspoon lemon peel

2 cups flour
2 tablespoons baking powder
½ teaspoon salt
½ teaspoon baking soda
½ teaspoon nutmeg
½ teaspoon cinnamon
1 cup grated zucchini
½ cup chopped pecans
vegetable cooking spray

Preheat oven to 350°. With electric mixer, combine apple sauce, apple juice concentrate, fructose, oil, eggs, lemon juice and vanilla. Beat until well-blended. In a separate bowl, combine lemon peel, flour, baking powder, salt, baking soda, nutmeg and cinnamon. Add zucchini and nuts to dry mixture.

Add batter to dry mixture and blend well. Pour into 9" x 5" x 3" pan which has been coated with cooking spray. Bake for one hour or until inserted knife comes out clean.

Hint for the weight conscious:
Eat all the foods you can't stand.

PS. 32:1 TLB
What happiness for those whose guilt has been forgiven! What joys when sins are covered over! What relief for those who have confessed their sins and God has cleared their record!

Jogging may add years to our life. In fact,
you could feel 10 years older the first time you try it.

LOW FAT CHOCOLATE MUFFINS

¾ cup sugar
¾ cup cocoa
1½ teaspoons
  baking powder
½ teaspoon baking soda
3 large egg whites

¼ teaspoon salt
1 cup *plus*
  2 tablespoons flour
2 teaspoons vanilla
½ cup applesauce
½ cup buttermilk

Preheat oven to 350°. Coat 12 muffin tins with nonstick
cooking spray. In a large mixing bowl, combine the sugar,
flour, cocoa, baking powder, baking soda and salt. Blend well
using a wire whisk. Make a well in the center. In a separate
bowl, whisk egg whites with vanilla, applesauce and water.
Add to flour mixture. Stir just until blended. Do not overmix.
Spoon into prepared muffin tins. Bake 25 minutes or until a
toothpick comes out clean. Cool on wire rack 15 minutes
before removing from pan.

JOHN 3:16–17

For God so loved the world, that he gave his only
begotten son, that whosoever believeth in him
should not perish, but have everlasting life.
For God sent not his Son into the world
to condemn the world:
but that the world through Him might be saved.

THE SECRET OF METHUSELAH

Methuselah ate what he found on his plate
And never, as people do now,
Did he note the amount of the calorie count
He ate it because it was chow.

He wasn't disturbed as at dinner he sat
Devouring a roast or a pie
To think it was lacking in granular fat
Or a couple of vitamins shy.

He cheerfully chewed each species of food,
Unmindful of troubles or fears
Lest his health might be hurt
By some fancy dessert
And he lived over 900 years.

Penny Scales

"It's Up to You"

Have you made someone happy
or made someone sad,
What have you done with the
day that you had?
God gave it to you
to do as you would.
Did you do what was wicked,
or do what was good?
Did you hand out a smile, or
Just give 'em a frown.
Did you lift someone up, or
push someone down?
Did you lighten some load, or
some progress impede,
Did you look for a rose, or
just gather a weed?
What did you do with your
beautiful day,
God gave it to you, did you
throw it away?

Kid
Stuff

Twin Grandsons, Bryan and Ryan

SAY IT WITH FLOWERS
A rose can say I love you,
Orchids can enthrall;
But a weed bouquet in a chubby fist,
Oh my, that says it all!

SCRAMBLED EGGS

2 eggs	1 tablespoon butter
3 tablespoons milk	salt

Break eggs into small bowl. Add small amount of salt. Add milk and beat together with whisk or fork until mixed well. Put butter into pan and melt on medium heat. Spread butter over pan to keep eggs from sticking. Add beaten eggs and stir with spatula until eggs are light and fluffy. Enjoy!

FRENCH TOAST

Usually a treat for breakfast.

1 egg	1 tablespoon butter
2 slices bread	3 tablespoons milk

Beat egg and milk together. Melt butter in frying pan over medium heat. When pan is hot, dip slice of bread into egg mixture, coating both sides. Place in frying pan and cook on both sides until light brown. Place on plate and serve with syrup. You may want to double or triple recipe.

Once upon a memory, someone wiped away a tear ♡ Held me close and loved me ♡ Thank you, Mother dear.

DEVILED EGGS

A necessary treat for children.

hard boiled eggs　　**salad dressing** *or*
salt　　**mayonnaise**
pickle relish　　**a little mustard**

Peel eggs and cut in half lengthwise. Remove yolk carefully, so the egg won't tear. Place in bowl and mash with a fork. Add salt to taste, mustard, pickle relish and enough salad dressing to make moist consistency. Refill egg whites. Garnish with a sprinkle of paprika.

To be in your children's memories tomorrow, you have to be in their lives today.

GRILLED CHEESE SANDWICH

A child pleaser for lunch!

1 slice American cheese　　**mayonnaise** *or*
2 pieces bread　　**salad dressing,**
butter　　**optional**

If using mayonnaise, spread over bread lightly. Place one slice of cheese between the pieces of bread. Spread butter on outside of bread and place in frying pan on medium heat. Brown both sides. Mash down lightly with spatula as it is cooking.

A hug is better than all the theology in the world.

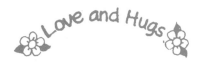

Grand-
daughter
Roxanne

STRAWBERRY CAKE

Wonderful for a birthday cake...fun to make!
Delicious!

1 Duncan Hines
yellow cake mix
whipped cream,

sweetened strawberries
sugar

Grease and flour two 9" cake pans. Bake cake as directed on package. Cool and cut layers into. Carefully put on wax paper, making 4 layers. Assemble together each layer with whipped cream and fresh sweetened strawberries, or frozen thawed strawberries, drained, over the whipped cream on each layer. Arrange whole or strawberry halves across top of cake to add beauty.

Note: Real whipping cream, is best to use...make someone happy today!

Jesus loves me,
this I know
for the Bible tells me so.

BLACK COW

1 **tall glass**   **cola**
3 **scoops ice cream,**   **straw**
   vanilla *or* **chocolate**

Put ice cream into tall glass. Fill glass with cola. Stir and serve. 7 Up is also delicious instead of cola.

*"Would you mind running through those
flavors just once more?"*

I KNOW I'M SOMEBODY 'cause God don't make no junk!!

OUR FAVORITE RECIPE

Children and Moms love this recipe.

2 **well scrubbed kids**   1 **fist full of dough**
1 **buttered-up daddy**

Place in well greased car and head for the nearest restaurant.

FUN JELLO

Great for car trips and parties.

4 **packages plain gelatin**   4 **cups boiling water**
3 **small packages Jello,**
any flavor

In a bowl, mix gelatin and Jello. Add boiling water and stir very well. Pour into 9" x 13" pan that has been sprayed with nonstick spray. Refrigerate until firm. Cut into squares.

Granddaughter Brittany

HUMPTY DUMPTY'S EGGNOG

1 egg	1 tablespoon
1 cup milk	powered sugar
cinnamon *or* nutmeg	1 teaspoon vanilla

Break egg into a medium size mixing bowl. Add the sugar and beat mixture with a fork to blend well. Add the milk and vanilla. Pour into a glass and sprinkle cinnamon on top.

Note: Children will probably prefer cinnamon. Store any leftovers in the refrigerator.

STEVE'S RED PUNCH

Inexpensive and very flavorful!

1 envelope	1 gallon apple juice
pre-sweetened cherry	
flavored drink mixture	

Dissolve drink mixture in apple juice. Chill before serving.

🐛 SUCCESS 🐛

You can use most any measure
When you're speaking of success.
You can measure it in fancy home,
Expensive car or dress.
But the measure of your real success
Is the one you cannot spend.
It's the way your kids describe you
When they're talking to a friend.

EGG SALAD SANDWICHES

Tasty for big kids too!
Triple recipe for party sandwiches.

3 hard boiled eggs
salt to taste
2 tablespoons
pickle relish

2 tablespoons
salad dressing *or*
mayonnaise

Peel eggs and place in a bowl. Mash with a fork until in very small pieces. Add rest of ingredients and mix well.

"You know you're having a bad day when you put the dirty clothes to bed and the kids in the hamper."

QUICK PIZZAS

Children love these!

hamburger buns
1 jar pizza sauce

ground chuck
mozzarella cheese

Preheat oven to 350°. Brown meat in pan. Add pizza sauce to meat and mix well. Split buns and spoon sauce on each half. Sprinkle with grated cheese. Place on a cookie sheet. Bake until cheese is melted. These are a big hit at parties.

You can get children off your lap,
but you can never get them out of your heart.

REESE CUP COOKIES

Always a children's favorite. Yummy!

1 package refrigerator   **miniature Reese Cups**
chocolate chip cookies

Bake chocolate chip cookies according to package directions. Remove cookies from oven, placing on wax paper. Put a Reese Cup in the center of each cookie.

Grandchildren Roxanne, Amy,
Nathan, Ryan and Bryan

SMILING PANCAKE FACES

Enjoy making these fun pancakes
with your children.

Using your favorite pancake mix, follow directions on label. Then pour batter into large cookie cutters, frying in a medium heated skillet. Do not fry to fast. A teflon skillet is great to use. Do not use to much batter.

Note: Do not forget to butter the pancakes...and hot syrup over pancakes makes them complete...will make you smile!

HELP!

In church last Sunday, the congregation was treated to the loud antics of a boy no more than four. After several attempts to silence him, the chagrined father began hauling the youngster across the row and down the long aisle to the rear of the church. The situation looked dire until, suddenly, a light gleamed in the boy's eyes.

To the crowds happy cheers and guffaws, the boy began gleefully shouting words he had been taught to yell if being abducted: "This man is not my father! Help me! This man is not my father!"

PORCUPINE MEAT BALLS

1 cup bread crumbs
1 pound ground chuck
1 egg
1 tablespoon
  parsley flakes
⅓ cup uncooked rice
1 teaspoon
  seasoning salt
¼ cup brown sugar

2 teaspoons
  worcestershire sauce
¾ teaspoon salt
1 tablespoon
  minced onion
1 8 ounce can
  tomato sauce
1 cup water

In a mixing bowl, combine the ground chuck, bread crumbs, egg, worcestershire sauce, salt, parsley flakes and minced onion. Mix together and form beef into 8 meatballs. Roll each meatball in the rice so that the rice sticks to it. Put the rice in a skillet. Make the sauce by combining the brown sugar, tomato sauce and seasoning salt. Pour this sauce over each meatball. Carefully pour the water into the skillet between the meatballs, not over them. Cover the skillet with a lid and simmer over medium heat for about 45 minutes.

MOTHER'S COVERS
When you were small
And just a touch away,
I covered you with blankets
Against the cool night air.
But now that you are tall
And out of reach,
I fold my hands
And cover you with prayer.

TUNA BURGER

1 7 ounce can tuna	soft butter
½ cup grated	1 teaspoon
cheddar cheese	minced onion
dash black pepper	½ teaspoon celery salt
1 teaspoon	¼ cup mayonnaise
worcestershire sauce	3 english muffins

Have an adult help with this recipe. In a bowl, flake the tuna with a fork and combine it with rest of ingredients, then split the English muffins in half and spread inside lightly with butter. Pile the tuna mixture on top of each muffin half*. Wrap each muffin half in aluminum foil and place on a baking sheet. Bake for 15 minutes in a 350° oven.

Use favorite cookie cutters for children's sandwiches for a special treat.

Grandson
Clay

CLAY'S EGGS & CHEESE

Even a treat for supper!

2 eggs	2 slices cheese

In a skillet melt a small amount of butter. With Mom's help, put egg in skillet, break yolk and fry on medium heat until ready to turn over. After turning over, melt slice of cheese on each egg. Serve with toast and jelly. YUMMY!

TRUE GEMS

From Children

Pam's mother asked her how she liked her first day at school. Pam replied, "I don't like my teacher." Her mother asked her why and she said, "All day long all she does is kid stuff."

Three year old Kelly's hair had just got long enough for a pony tail when she cut it. She was asked why she did it and she replied, "Because I wanted to look like Daddy."

Four year old Loran was in the car seat and the sun was beaming in on her and she replied, "Momma, turn the sun down."

Debbie was teaching at the same school that her son Zach went to. Debbie asked him how he liked the fire drill. The son replied, "I didn't see it, the teacher made us go outside."

Grandma Jane was babysitting with her grandson Clay, and he looked at her and said, "Grandma, did you used to be pretty?" His big brother Clifton looked at him and said, "Clay, Grandma was a cheerleader three years in high school." (Big brother coming to Grandma Jane's rescue to console her!)

Grandma Mary had fallen over her Grandson's bicycle and had broken her arm. It was in a cast. On their way to church Mike asked her why she didn't have any wrinkles on her hand. Grandma explained that when she had fallen, her hand had swollen which caused the skin to be smooth. Mike replied, "Maybe you can fall on your face sometime..."

Bruce had gone to a wedding with his parents and when he saw the bride he said, "Is that Cinderella?"

Eric was looking in his grand-mother's annual and asked her which picture was hers. He picked the right picture and was asked how he had found her. He said, "I just picked the prettiest girl." (That sure might win some brownie points. Ha!)

Austin had seen a dead squirrel in the road. He replied, "He didn't look both ways."

Jane was babysitting with four of her grandchildren. Adam, Erica and Andy decided to play house. Adam being the daddy, Erica, the mother and Andy was the baby. Adam, being the daddy said, "I'm going to work." Erica, the mother said, "No way, I'm going to work and I'm not taking the baby to the babysitters..."

Ryan was spending a few days with his grandparents and had done something that displeased his Grandma Jane and she threatened to tell his dad. Ryan spoke up and said, "God doesn't keep track of wrongs."

A little girl told her mother that she was running away, so her mother helped her pack her clothes. She went outside and was sitting on the curb. Someone came along and asked her what she was doing and that little girl replied, "I'm running away, but I can't cross the street."

The prayer had been prayed, thanking the Lord for the food when Jerry said, "What is he...a Landlord?"

When Jim was a little tike, he enjoyed telling this joke. A little boy went to a pet store and asked the clerk, "Mither, can I buy some burrd theed?" The clerk answered, "Come back when you can talk plainer." The little boy returned the next day, saying to the clerk, "Mither, could I buy some buurd theed?" The clerk again answered, "Come back when you can talk plainer." This went on repeatedly for a few days. The little boy went back to the pet store and asked the clerk, "Mither, would you like to buy a dead bird?"

Nathan told this joke, of a man whose name was Odd. All through his life he did not like his name and said when he died there would be no name on his tombstone. So when he died there was nothing on his tombstone. When people would go by it, they would say, "Well, that's odd."

When Clifton was three years old, his Grandpa put up a swing for him. Grandpa asked Clifton if he was Grandpa's boy. Clifton answered, "No, I'm my dad's boy." Grandpa told him that he would take down the swing. Clifton answered, "Just take it down, Grandpa."

I was teaching the four year old Sunday School class, and I asked the children what they would like to sing. Judson replied, "There goes a bulldozer, that's serious."

Four year old Judson had stayed with a babysitter and she warned him, if he wasn't good, that she would spank him. He looked at her and said, "You're quite a woman."

Twins Dawn and Donna lived across the street from school and they had gone home for lunch and was ready to return to school. One said to the other, "Wait on me, my boyfriend will think you are me."

JUST FOR FUN

Children Chuckles

Father to son, "How was your report card?"
Son: "Well, I did the same thing as George Washington. I went down in History."

Q: Do you know who invented fractions?
A: Henry the 8th.

"My dog counts," said Tommy. Johnny asked, "How do you know that?" "Well, I asked him what 2 minus 2 was and he said nothing."

Q: Do you know what the grape said when the elephant sat down on him?
A: He didn't say anything, he just gave out a little wine.

Q: Why did the fellow take a ladder to the ballgame with him?
A: Because he heard the Giants were playing.

Dick: "I've eaten beef all my life and now I am strong as a bull.
Dan: "That's funny, I've been eating fish for a long time and I can't swim a stroke."

Q: Do you know what they call a cow with no feet?
A: Ground beef.

Have you heard about the bed? It hasn't been made up yet.

Singing "Chiquita Banana Song"
with grandson Clifton

Have you heard about the sidewalk? It's all over town.

One day a man was lost in the hills of Tennessee and he stopped and asked a little boy how he got to Memphis. The little boy replied, "My Dad takes me."

Q: What did they call a cat that fell into a computer?
A: A copy cat.

A little boy came home from Sunday School real excited that he had received a part in the Christmas play. His mother asked which part. He replied, "I'm one of the three wise guys."

Q: What do you have if you keep pet ducks in a box?
A: A box of quackers.

Q: What two words in a dentist's office can make a toothache go away?
A: "You're next."

"Dad, I think I'm failing mathematics." "Son, you've got to be more positive." "Well, I know I'm failing Math."

FOR MOMS

"I can't believe school starts tomorrow!"

Ode to VBS

My dishes went unwashed today,
I didn't make the bed,
I took God's hand and followed
To VBS instead.

Oh, yes, we went adventuring,
The children and I,
Exploring the whole Bible,
For truths we can't deny.

My house was sure neglected,
And I didn't sweep the stair,
In twenty years no one on earth
Will know, or even care.

But that I've helped a boy or girl
To noble adulthood grow,
In twenty years the whole wide world
May look, and see, and know!

FOR MOMS

Run the vacuum often — not to clean, but to drown out the kids.

🍇

Little boy's letter to his grandmother: "Dear Grandma: I'm sorry I forgot your birthday last week. It would serve me right if you forgot mine next Tuesday."

> 🍇
>
> To laugh often
> and much,
> to win the respect
> of intelligent people
> and the affection
> of children,
> to leave the world
> a bit better,
> to know even one life
> has breathed easier
> because you have lived,
> that is to have succeeded.

🍇

Kids are like sponges...they absorb all your strength and leave you limp. Give 'em a squeeze and you get it all back.

There was a lady standing on the street corner with several children, when a lady came up to her and said, "Oh, is this a Sunday School picnic?" The mother said, "No, these are all my children and it's no picnic."

🍇

A fellow was talking to a friend, and in essence of conversation said, "Oh, by the way, did I tell you about my Grandchildren?" His friend replied, "No, you didn't and I really appreciate it!"

🍇

A man was in a grocery store and among other things he had in the cart was a screaming baby. He was hurrying down the aisles shopping and repeating to himself, "Stay calm Albert, don't get excited Albert, don't yell Albert." A lady watching said, "My, you are to be commended for trying to quiet Albert." He replied, "Lady, I am Albert."

🍇

The greatest work you will ever do will be within the walls of your own home.

Being a parent means you spend the first two years teaching a kid how to walk and talk, and the next eighteen years trying to teach him to sit down and be quiet.

Bumper Sticker: Have you hugged your child today?

"I was thinking of doing what Hannah did — you recall she took her kid to the church and left him there!"

If a woman's place is in the home, why am I always in the car?

A mother invited several people for dinner and she had ended up with a very exhausting day with several unplanned things crowding into her day, but she had the meal prepared and she and her family, along the the company were seated around the table. She turned to her daughter and asked her to return thanks. The daughter replied, "I don't know what to say." The mother told her to just pray like she had. So the little girl bowed her head and prayed, "Dear Lord, why did I invite all these people over here tonight?"

I here are three ways to get something done: do it yourself, hire someone to do it, or forbid you kids to do it.

Serenity Prayer

God grant me
the serenity
to accept the things
I cannot change,
Courage enough
to change
the things I can,
and Wisdom
to know the difference.

❦ Thank You, Dear God ❦

Thank you, dear God, for dirty socks on the floor,
For finger-printed windows and wide-open doors,
For unmade beds and dirty dishes to do,
For sniffles and sneezes and sunburn and flu.

Thank you, dear God, for the dust everywhere,
And the large grape stain on my favorite chair,
For gum on shoe soles and tracks in the hall,
And the shattered window where Scott threw his ball.

Thank you, dear God, for bruises and cuts,
And the day that Charlie got choked on the nuts,
For torn jeans to sew and dirty floors to mop,
And my enormous bill when I grocery shop.

Thank you, dear God, for all of these things,
Even my furniture with large water rings;
For I know that without them I'd be alone,
And without a family to call all my own.

—Marietta C. Reed

F O O D

For Thought

A good outfit can cure a bad day.

Keep a Journal. Record those inspirational things that have brought you a bubble of joy. You will have things to inspire you when you need a lift. You know, on days when hair spray is the only thing holding you together...

Arrange a corner in your home just for you. We need our space, where we can call it our own place to meditate, where we can spend time alone to be renewed, and refreshed, where we write that letter we intended to write last month. I like a statement by Barbara Johnson, "Where we can feel God's comfort blanket of love around us."

Life is a grindstone. But whether it grinds us down or polishes us up depends on us.

A successful woman seeks and finds that which is beautiful in all people...and all things: whose heart is full of love and warm with compassion, who has found joy in living and peace within herself...who puts her best into each task and does her best to make situations better than she found them.

Simplify your life. Learn what is important and what is not...learn to say no to situations that have no worth. Celebrate one day a month doing something for yourself.

Take time to smell the roses.

Read, write, relax.

To Thyself be true.

JUST FOR FUN

Laughing is the Best Medicine!

A man ran down three flights of stairs to answer the telephone. He grabbed the phone and said hello. The voice on the other end said, "Sorry, wrong number." The fellow, out of breath, said, "That's okay, I had to answer the phone anyway."

A lady thought she recognized the man who had sold her a car and said to him, "Are you the fellow who sold me this car two weeks ago?" The salesman said 'yes' very proudly. "Well, tell me about it again, I get so discouraged."

An advertisement company ad read, "Let us stick your nose in our business."

Hey waiter, do you have frog legs?" "No, I've always walked this way."

Did you hear about the cross-eyed school teacher who couldn't control her pupils?

A man was mailing a Bible at the post office and the clerk asked if there was anything breakable in the package. He replied, "Only the Ten Commandments."

The Pastor told his congregation if they wanted to donate $400.00 to please stand up, then told the organist to play The Star Spangled Banner.

A man had just spoke somewhere with a portable speaker and it rattled terrible. Afterward, the master of ceremonies said, "I want to apologize for our speaker, there must be a screw loose somewhere."

Did you hear about the fellow who ran through a screen door and strained himself?

Young
at
Heart

TEMPERATURES

Oven & Meat Thermometer

OVEN

Temperature Fahrenheit	Term
250° – 300°	Slow
325°	Moderately slow
350°	Moderate
375°	Moderately quick
400°	Moderately hot
425° – 450°	Hot
475° – 500°	Extremely hot

MEAT THERMOMETER

Beef
Rare	140°
Medium	160°
Well-done	170°

Fresh Pork   170° – 185°

Smoke Pork
Fully Cooked	130°
Cook-before eating	160°

Veal   170°

Lamb   175° – 180°

YOUNG

At Heart

*We underestimate
the value of laughter!*
—*Henry Wadsworth Longfellow*

PROVERBS 17:22
"A merry heart doeth good like a medicine: but a broken spirit drieth the bones."

Happiness is contagious
...be a carrier.

If you are happy, I wish you would notify your face.

IT FACED A BLANK WALL!
The pursuit of happiness is a matter of choice — it is a positive attitude we choose to express. It is NOT a gift delivered to our door each morning, nor does it come through a window. It is certain that our circumstances are not the things that make our lives complete. If we wait for life to get just right, we will never laugh again!

WARNING!
Laughter may be hazardous to your illness.

*You do have a choice —
be happy!*

A ROCKING CHAIR IS GOOD FOR YOUR HEART
Sitting in that old rocking chair can be good for your health as you age.

A study of 25 people age 65 to 95 showed that rocking in a rocking chair is a mild but effective exercise for the heart, according to a report in the Medical Abstracts Newsletter.

You know you're getting old when you stoop to tie your shoes and wonder what else you can do while you're down there.

❧

Life begins at forty — if you think rheumatism is living.

❧

You don't stop laughing because you grow old...you grow old because you stop laughing.

❧

There is always a lot to be thankful for if you take time to look for it. Right now, I am sitting here thinking how nice it is that wrinkles don't hurt.

❧

My mind not only wanders, sometimes it leaves completely.

"I live in the future, not the past. Each day I plan what I am going to do the next day, and today is already half over."

❧

My memory is excellent. There are only three things I can't remember. I can't remember faces, I can't remember names, and... I have forgotten the third thing.

❧

Ooh... you smell so good... what do you have on? Ben–Gay.

❧

It's hard to be nostalgic when you can't remember anything. When your memory goes...forget it!

Did you know —
Senior Citizens are
the biggest carriers
of AIDS???
Hearing Aids
Band-Aids
Rol-Aids
Walking-Aids
Medic-Aids

Things to do today:
1. Get up.
2. Survive.
3. Go to bed.

Usher: "How far down do
you wish to sit?"
Sweet little old lady: "All
the way down, I'm so tired."

Saw a little cartoon with an
old may saying to a friend,
"At my age, I realize I've
already said everything I
ever wanted to say, so from
here on out, I'll just be
repeating myself."

*"My face in the mirror
Isn't wrinkled or drawn.
My furniture is dusted;
The cobwebs are gone.
My garden is lovely
And so is my lawn.
I don't thing I will ever
Put my glasses back on..."*

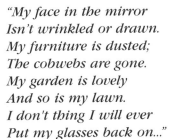

"I think we need to learn how to communicate with each other more effectively. If you agree with me, grunt once. If you disagree, grunt twice."

"You bet. Retirement is great."

"He's napping right now, but I'll tell him you called when he gets up to go to bed."

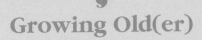

Growing Old(er)

Dear Lord,
I don't much like growing old(er).
My eyesight isn't great,
Nor my hearing,
Nor my balance,
Nor my arthritis,
But I realize that's all negative.
I can still read;
I have a hearing aid;
I have my cane;
I have Ben-Gay;
And, praise the Lord,
I can still praise the Lord!

But I still don't much like
growing old(er).

by: Beatrice B. MacAlpine

How Am I? Well...

There is nothing the matter with me.
I'm as healthy as I can be.
I have arthritis in both of my knees,
And when I talk, I talk with a wheeze.
My pulse is weak and my blood is thin,
But I'm awfully well for the shape I'm in.

Arch supports I have for my feet,
Or I wouldn't be able to be on the street.
Sleep is denied me, night after night,
But every morning I find I'm alright.
My memory is failing, my head's in a spin,
But I'm awfully well for the shape I'm in.

The moral is this, as this tale unfolds,
That for me and you who are growing old.
It's better to say, "I'm fine" with a grin,
Than to let folks know the shape we're in.

How do I know that my youth is all spent?
Well, my "getup and go" has got up and went.
But I really don't mind when I think with a grin,
Of all the grand places my "get up" has been.

Old age is golden, I've heard it said,
But sometimes I wonder as I get into bed.
With my ears in the drawer, my teeth in a cup,
My eyes on the table until I wake up.

I get up each morning and dust off my wits,
Pick up the papers and read the obits.
If my name is still missing, I know I'm not dead,
So I get a good breakfast and go back to bed.

—Anonymous

Things Just Ain't The Same Anymore

Everything is further away than it used to be.
It is twice as far to the corner,
and I notice that they've added a hill.

I've given up running for the bus.
It leaves faster than it used to.

It seems they're making the stairs steeper
than in the old days, too.
And have you noticed the smaller print
they now use in the newspaper?

There is no sense in asking anyone to read aloud —
everyone speaks in such low voices
I can hardly hear them.

The material in clothes — so skimpy now —
especially around the waist.
It's almost impossible to reach my shoelaces
and I can't figure out why!

Even people are changing.
They are so much younger than they used to be,
when I was their age.
On the other hand,
people my own age are too much older than I am.
I ran across an old classmate the other day,
and he had aged so badly he didn't recognize me!!!

—Author unknown

INDEX

May the road rise up to meet you,
May the wind always be at your back.
May the sunshine be warm upon your face,
And the rain fall softly upon your fields.
And until we meet again,
May God hold in the hollow of thy hand.

NUMBERS 6:24–26
May the Lord bless you and keep you,
The Lord make his face to shine upon you,
And be gracious unto you.
The Lord lift up his countenance upon you
and give you peace.

Live Well
Laugh Often
Love Much

Love and Hugs
To You

FOOD, FUN & LAUGHTER
Mary Jane Remole ❦ P.O. Box 70593 ❦ Marietta, GA 30007

Please send me_____ copies of Food, Fun & Laughter @ $15.95 each $_____
Plus postage and handling @ $ 2.75 each $_____
TOTAL $_____

Ship to:
Name: _____

Street Address: _____

City/State/Zip: _____

FOOD, FUN & LAUGHTER
Mary Jane Remole ❦ P.O. Box 70593 ❦ Marietta, GA 30007

Please send me_____ copies of Food, Fun & Laughter @ $15.95 each $_____
Plus postage and handling @ $ 2.75 each $_____
TOTAL $_____

Ship to:
Name: _____

Street Address: _____

City/State/Zip: _____

FOOD, FUN & LAUGHTER
Mary Jane Remole ❦ P.O. Box 70593 ❦ Marietta, GA 30007

Please send me_____ copies of Food, Fun & Laughter @ $15.95 each $_____
Plus postage and handling @ $ 2.75 each $_____
TOTAL $_____

Ship to:
Name: _____

Street Address: _____

City/State/Zip: _____